I love going to casting sessions. Maybe it's because I'm not sure if actors are the bravest people on earth—or the craziest. As a writer, I could never imagine doing my craft in front of a group of people, especially strangers. I would absolutely freeze...plus, I prefer to deal with any rejection from the comfort of my own home. But, hey, this book isn't about me, it's about you, so read on and you will learn the Do's and Don'ts of auditioning. Ellie and Denny have written an informative and inspiring book that will give you insight into what's expected of you and what you can expect at an audition: It will do everything except get you the job. That, you'll have to do yourself. Good luck, or, as you brave (and/or) crazy people prefer: Break a leg.

—Constance Burge,
Creator of *Charmed*;
Writer for *Ed, Boston Public,*
Ally McBeal

How ^NOT^ to
AUDITION

Avoiding
The
Common
Mistakes
Most
Actors
Make

Ellie Kanner and Denny Martin Flinn

HOW NOT TO AUDITION
Avoiding the Common Mistakes Most Actors Make
Copyright © 2003 Ellie Kanner and Denny Martin Flinn

LONE EAGLE PUBLISHING COMPANY
1024 N. Orange Dr.
Hollywood, CA 90038
Phone 323.308.3400 or 800.815.0503
A division of IFILM® Corporation, www.hcdonline.com

Printed in the United States of America
10 9 8 7 6 5 4 3 2 1

Cover design by Lindsay Albert and Sheri Lam
Book design by Carla Green

Library of Congress Cataloging-in-Publication Data

Kanner, Ellie
      How not to audition : avoiding the common mistakes most actors make / Ellie Kanner, Denny Martin Flinn
            p.   cm. — (Next!)
      ISBN 1-58065-049-X
      1. Acting—Auditions. I. Flinn, Denny Martin. II. Title. III. Series.

PN2071.A92K34 2003

                                        2003054672

Breakdowns supplied by Breakdown Services, Ltd., Used with permission.

Books may be purchased in bulk at special discounts for promotional or educational purposes. Special editions can be created to specifications. Inquiries for sales and distribution, textbook adoption, foreign language translation, editorial, and rights and permissions inquiries should be addressed to: Jeff Black, Lone Eagle Publishing, 1024 N. Orange Drive, Hollywood, CA 90038 or send e-mail to info@ifilm.com.

Distributed to the trade by National Book Network, 800-462-6420.
IFILM® and Lone Eagle Publishing Company™ are registered trademarks.

Contents

Acknowledgments

All of the knowledge and experience I have to share on this subject is a direct result of my interaction with the thousands of
actors who have auditioned for me over the years. In a very real
sense, I am simply passing along lessons they have taught me. They
have kept my job exciting and challenging, and their talent and
courage inspires me every day.

I might not have undertaken this book if not for the support of
Lone Eagle, particularly Jeff Black, who suggested the project;
Carla Green, who created a terrific layout; and Lauren Rossini, who
had great notes and guided me through the entire process. Many
thanks to Paul Bens for co-writing my first book, *NEXT! An Actor's
Guide to Auditioning.* A very special thanks to Denny Martin Flinn,
whose *How NOT to Write a Screenplay* was the model for this book.
I am honored he agreed to work with me, and any impression one
may have that this book is well written is entirely his doing.

A number of talented colleagues and friends contributed to
this book, in many cases without attribution. They all deserve top
billing on a separate card above the title. Since that's not possible,
I'll list them alphabetically. They are: Scott Baio, Connie Burge,
K Callan, Steve LaManna, Matt LeBlanc, Kathleen Letterie, Traci
Lords, Gary Marsh, Ivana Milicevic, Steve Pearlman, Lloyd Segan,
Greg Serano, Bob Stevens, Paul Stupin and Dori Zuckerman. You all
have my heartfelt thanks and appreciation.

On a more personal level, my parents, Sid and Shirley, and my
sister, Susan, deserve mention. I can never repay them for a life-

time of love and encouragement, but I can put their names in the front of this book, and that's a start.

Thanks also to my husband, David, for his love and support. He is my best friend and a man of immense talent. I will always appreciate his help in rewriting these acknowledgments. (In fact, those last two sentences were all his.) And finally, thanks to my eight week-old son, *Zachary*, for permitting me to work on this book when I should have been nursing him and changing his diaper. C'mon, kiddo, it's time to eat.

Introduction

There are three plateaus in an actor's career.

First, to get paid for what you do. You can't focus much on your art if you're waiting tables day and night to pay the rent.

Second, to have your work known among your peers, particularly casting directors, directors and producers. That will bring you wider opportunities.

Third, to have your work known by the general public, which can give you leverage with producers, studios and networks.

The first plateau is the highest and hardest, and you've got to audition well to reach it.

This book is for young actors, many of whom arrive in New York and Hollywood every season with a strong background in acting and years of experience doing plays in high school and college, but without the foggiest idea of how to go about getting a job.

Obviously, you're not alone. The universal success of *A Chorus Line*—the Broadway musical about dancers auditioning for a Broadway musical—illustrates the proverb: "Life is an audition." Many people outside the theatre identified with the young dancers putting their talent, their skill and, most revealing of all, their egos, on the line. Whether it's for a Broadway musical or a corporate job, a cheerleading squad or a spot in college, everybody auditions. A speech is an audition. A blind date is an audition. Everybody is selling something.

For actors, the product is you.

Let's begin with something you probably don't know (and might find hard to believe):

The people on the other side of the table are not your enemy.

This is important to remember. Rejection after rejection of your great talent can tend to thicken your skin. That's unavoidable, and necessary in the acting business. It can gradually encourage you to resent the agents, casting directors, producers, directors, studio and network executives who turned you down. How dare they?

Let's look at it from their point of view. What they're waiting for, hoping for, dying for, is the actor to walk in and blow them away with his or her reading. These people admire creative talent—especially those who have none of their own, and have to wear suits. Agents are desperate to sign the next big thing. Casting directors know that their next job depends on doing this one well. Any good director knows that directing is never less than 51 percent casting, sometimes a lot more. Writers don't really want to hear what they've been hearing in their head for a year, they want it to be taken further. They want to look up and say, "*Wow, it's alive!*" People who are casting are digging for gold. So, believe it or not...

They're on your side.

But only for a few minutes. That's how long you've got to make an impression. First, it's a question of your physical type. There's nothing you can do about that (although we'll talk more about "looking the part" in Chapter 10). Depending on how close you are to being right for the part, you're either going to be seriously considered, or just allowed the brief courtesies and ushered out the door. Sometimes, for commercials, they may never let you read at all. Film, theatre and TV will usually let you read. However, don't always think it was your reading that got the "Thank you, next." Good as you read, you may not fit their pre-conceived notion of the role. It's the almost daily job of an actor to schlep to auditions of one kind or another. Even big stars have to read for a director sometimes. Don't get discouraged if you get a quick brush-off. There's a prototype for the role, and they had to take a look to see if you fit. You didn't. Not your fault.

Every veteran director has experienced two phenomenon. One is the actor who delivers a brilliant audition but never gets any further with the role, and may even get bogged down (usually by over-intellectualizing) in rehearsals until he's worse. The second is the actor who gives a terrible audition, but is brilliant in the part, having gotten it because the director knew him, "had an instinct," or because no one else was available. In the former case, the actor's readings are usually a little too slick and stagy, lacking in sincerity, as if they've played the same part many times already (which probably they have, given the prevalence of type casting in Hollywood). The latter actor is either far too nervous to produce— for many actors, auditions are more nerve-wracking than performances—or working through some kind of "method," and doesn't want to arrive at his destination too soon.

• • •

Director: You're the wrong height.

Actor: I can be taller.

Director: You don't understand. We're looking for someone shorter.

Actor: I don't have to be this tall. Look, I'm wearing lifts. I can be shorter.

Director: I know, but we're looking for somebody different.

Actor: I can be different.

Director: We're looking for somebody else, okay?

—*Tootsie*, Columbia Pictures, 1982

• • •

Ideally, you don't want to get caught in either category. The actor who gives lousy auditions isn't going to get booked very often, and may struggle for years to establish a decent reputation. The actor who doesn't grow in a role during rehearsals (if there are any rehearsals), risks getting fired.

In short, there are plenty of good actors out there who don't audition well. Unfortunately, the audition is such an intrinsic part of the business that you can be a brilliant actor and never get paid for it. That would be a shame.

If you're a good actor and a bad auditioner—a category it seems that a lot of actors feel they fit into—something is wrong. It just isn't natural for a good actor to give bad auditions. You're somehow blocked from delivering your best. It could be your audition technique. It could be your attitude. Either way, you've got to do something about it.

We've tried to break down potential behavior into various Do's and Don'ts, repeating the most important points at the end of each chapter. Our emphasis is on the Don'ts for a simple reason. We can't make you a good actor, but we can help your talent to shine through. We want you to be seen clearly, not behind a smoke screen of mistakes.

We'll be repeating two mantras throughout this book. The first is: *Use your common sense.* Behind the scenes, beyond *People* magazine, the entertainment business is not glamorous. There are wheelers and dealers, hucksters and hustlers, friends and enemies, potholes and pitfalls. Try to navigate a straight course, keep your balance, and behave admirably. The second is more specific: *Be prepared.* Performing is a rigorous craft. Never go to an audition less than well-prepared to do your very best.

> • • •
>
> An actor once read for a part in a film, then thanked the people before him, and turned to leave the room. "Wait," the director called out, "we want you for the film. We want you to play the part."
>
> "Oh, no thanks," said the actor. "I only do auditions."
>
> • • •

Just as every writer knows that every script sent out is a sample of his or her work, you should know that every audition is an opportunity to let people know how good you are, whether or not you're right for the current role. You want to make a strong impression. Casting directors in particular are always looking for new talent. If the same casting director has brought you in for numerous roles, and you haven't locked one of them, don't despair. She thinks you've got something, and is still looking for a good match. If a director has asked to see you several times, he or she would like to work with you. Just maybe not this time. Every audition is a chance to strut your stuff, to make fans of your talent. You'll want to be sharp, each and every time. Here's how...

> • • •
>
> Throughout this book, we have standardized the casting director as "she," rather than using the universal pronoun "he." Many, though by no means all, casting directors are women, and thus this small nod to equality. In fact, it can be noted that this is so simply because breaking into the casting business requires the slave wages and hours that more women than men are willing to put up with in today's still politically incorrect employment climate.
>
> • • •

1

A Few Words about the People Behind the Desk, or Out There in the Dark

THE AGENT

Few agents actually hold auditions. They'd prefer to see you work in a play, a film or a television show. If you're looking for an agent, and you've landed a part, send out a postcard or a letter inviting people to see you in it. You should invite any agents you've met, or you can use the scattershot approach, and target every legitimate agent in town. The unions have agreements with signatory agencies. Don't bother with anyone who isn't recognized by an actor's union. You don't have to be a union member to check their list of franchised agencies. Also, lists of these agencies and their contacts are published in several directories, available at any good film bookstore, including Larry Edmunds (the mother-of-all-great-film-bookstores in Hollywood), the Drama Book Shop (the mother-of-all-great-theatre-bookstores in Manhattan), and the ubiquitous (and well-stocked with film scripts, plays, and directories) Samuel French.

Even if you don't have tape of your work to show them, sometimes you can still get your foot in the door. Target new or small agencies. (Hint: *Variety* often reports on the latest assistants who have been promoted to full agent status, or the agent who has changed agencies and had to leave some of his clients behind.) Send them your picture and résumé with a nice brief note that you're new in town and you'd like to meet them. If they agree to see you, have a monologue prepared (see Chapter 17) in case they want to see you act. More likely, they'll just chat for a moment. At least you've made an impression. Even if all they do is say, "Let me know when you're in something," it's a start. Then, *get in something.* There are lots of small plays, student films, unpaid showcases and waiver-theatre productions around, and most of them hold open auditions, as they are desperate for actors who will work for free. As soon as you've scored a decent role, even if it's in a college production, re-send your photo (so they'll remember who you are), with a note reminding them that you met or spoke with them, and invite them to the show or screening.

• • •

While I was working at The Peter Strain Agency in New York, I flew up to Boston to visit my husband who was performing in a musical there. With nothing better to do, went the next night to see a little non-equity revue around the corner. It featured a young lady with all sorts of talent and charisma, and I went backstage to see her; her name was Faith Price. She didn't have an agent, so I gave her my card and told her to come see us if she ever decided to brave the Big Apple. A few months later she turned up at the office. We signed her, and within a few years she was starring in a Broadway musical and has since won a Tony Award! That was my most enjoyable success as an agent's assistant.

—Barbara Pearl

• • •

IF YOU'VE ALREADY GOT AN AGENT...

• Make sure he or she gets free tickets to any play you're in. Nothing is worse than finding out that your agent has lost interest in you months *after* he or she lost interest in you. Keep your agent excited about your talent.

• Make sure your agent has enough copies of your latest picture and résumé, and demo reel (see Chapter 3).

• For goodness sake, don't make an enemy of your agent's assistant. This isn't just a matter of good manners. Assistants are the ones who are going to be efficient (or not), about sending your stuff out. The assistant is probably going to be promoted shortly, and your agent's top clients are going to demand more and more of his time. Unless you're booking regularly, the person who asked if you wanted Perrier or Evian when you first came in could be responsible for your career one day soon.

- Never pay an agent or manager up front. Agents get 10 percent. That is, a percentage of the money they earn for you by putting you up for jobs and negotiating the contracts. Personal managers get 10 to 15 percent (and are legally prohibited from negotiating on your behalf). These percentages are set not only by the contracts you should have with your agent and/or manager, but by the performing unions involved, and in some cases by state law.
- Some agents may represent you in all fields—film, television, commercials, voice-overs, theatre—and would receive their commission on everything you earn in those fields. Others may only represent you in a single field or a specific medium. Before you sign with an agent, understand your specific relationship.

THE CASTING ASSOCIATE

Busy casting directors may have an associate in the office assigned to a particular show. Sometimes they'll be fully responsible for a show, and do all of the on-line casting. Sometimes they'll do just the pre-read, before passing them on to their boss...

THE CASTING DIRECTOR

Either way, the casting office is your first obstacle. Let's take a look at who these people are.

First, they're in the same desperate business you are. They need another job as soon as this one is over. They audition as well. For producers. They bring in their résumés, make lists for projects and share ideas for free in the hope of being hired.

Although they're the gatekeepers who are keeping you from fame and fortune, it might help to remember that they're almost as nervous as you. If they don't bring in a fair amount of talent for the producers to see, if they don't seem to have a handle on the roles to be cast, they're not going to work for that producer again or get a good recommendation. They're human, too. Many of them were actors or actresses at one time, and sympathize.

Casting directors almost never decide who is cast in a role. It's their job to present a number of appropriate actors for each role, in order to save the producer and director time. In Hollywood, a green light for a film project usually comes after months, even years, of "development." Then, all of a sudden, they want it yesterday. They've probably set a start date for principal photography, and worked backwards from there to establish the rest of the schedule. Suddenly the project is on a fast track, and the producer and director don't have time to sit through days and weeks of auditions, or have the patience to see everyone who wants to be seen. Enter the casting director, and the lists.

A word about lists. There are all sorts of actor lists in Hollywood. If a studio is going to spend 100 million dollars to make a picture, they're going to want an actor who has proved he can "open" a picture. This means that the actor's last picture, or at least a relatively recent one, had a strong box office on opening weekend. A star. Usually male, although Julia Roberts and a few other women have been able to crack that particular glass ceiling. If the studio is going to finance a smaller (lower budget) picture, they're still anxious to have a star commit—and after they approach the A-list actors and discover that their budget would be shot to hell even if the actor's agent would let him appear in a "smaller" picture, they'll go to the next list: actors who have been successful in leading roles on the independent feature circuit. Same with television. Most sitcoms and MOWs are built around a well-known performer, someone who's had a successful series already (Mary Tyler Moore, Kelsey Grammer, Ted Danson); or been successful on the stand-up comedy circuit (Jerry Seinfeld, Ellen DeGeneres, Ray Romano, Bernie Mac); or a well-known actor who is currently less in demand for features, yet still a celebrity (Candice Bergen, Bette Midler, Richard Dreyfuss, Kiefer Sutherland).

If you're on those lists, you don't need this book, you need an agent who can read and judge scripts, because you're going to be offered roles fairly consistently. And you'll want an agent who has his ear to the ground, because really good roles are rare, and you'll want to know about them pronto. Let's get to the lists *you* want to get on.

Casting directors are constantly going to plays and musicals, and constantly watching films and television shows. The essence of their job is to be aware of all the talent in the industry, the new, the up-and-coming, and the working actors. It's fairly easy to keep up with the working actors. The up-and-coming are more difficult to spot, and finding the good new actor is like looking for a needle in a haystack. Casting directors attend film festivals, because independent films boast young, hungry actors, any one of whom could be the next Parker Posey or Steve Buscemi. They scout plays in lofts and garages throughout the community, because that's where many actors get their start. It's a lot more fun, and a lot more informative, to see a show or watch a film than to ask an actor to come to your office and read. Not only can they check out more than one actor at a time, but it's the real thing. Watching a film or television show, a casting director looks for the supporting actors, even one-line bits, who make an impression. Those are the new people the casting director can help discover. A sharp casting director never forgets a good actor. You want a casting director to remember you when she is making her lists.

Don't pay to see a casting director. Casting directors get paid by the production. Good casting directors will see new actors in their spare time

• • •

So you wanna know more about auditions? Well, you'll have good and bad ones. That's a guarantee. Ones you think went well, didn't. Others where you think you tanked, you shined. All in all, you never know what the powers that be are looking for. Sure, your agent, manager or the list in Breakdown will give you a rough sketch of the role, but it's up to the actor to take the sketch, add the color, and pull it off the page.

Often your only ally in the audition situation is the casting director. The casting director is the liaison between you and the aforementioned powers that be. They know what they want. A few key words of advice on your way into the room can inspire confidence, give you insight, and help you tweak your adaptation of the role—enough so that, hopefully, you will be successful in keeping your rent paid.

Preparation is the key to an actor's job. Often, however, there is little or no time to prepare. Thus the importance to the actor of the casting director.

—Matt LeBlanc

P.S. Hey, Ellie, thanks again for the callback on *Friends*.

• • •

to make sure their files are up to date, because often, in television especially, there's very little time to cast some roles. Casting directors do this scouting on their own. And in any case, it's unethical, and in most cases, illegal, to charge actors to audition.

There are some casting directors who give "classes," "seminars," or "workshops." Don't sign up for them under the belief that you're getting in the door. Workshops, classes and seminars can teach an inexperienced actor a great deal, but there are plenty of snake-oil salesman in the entertainment industry, so do your homework. Check with actors who have taken the class. Was it worth it? Make sure it was a class where they learned something, and wasn't just a paid "audition." Some teachers will allow you to audit their classes.

The entertainment industry has a titanium door. Knocking on it politely doesn't usually do the trick. You've got to work at networking. And you've got to audition. There are no short cuts. But real industry professionals don't look to make money out of giving newcomers "access."

Legitimate jobs don't charge you, they pay you. A casting director who needs *you* to pay *her* is ripping you off and isn't one of the many legitimate casting directors in the industry. But the most important reason to avoid paying to see a casting director is that *you are belittling your own talent.* Try hard to remember this during the lean times: You're worth something.

As soon as a casting director is offered a project to cast, she is going to read the script carefully, then pitch herself to the producer. If the producer hires her, there is very little time to come up with names.

The casting director is probably going to have to spend a lot of time checking on the availability of the actors on the A-list for the leading roles. Hopefully she has a casting assistant who can do the grunt work, but she'll have to stay on top of what's happening. In other words...

There is even less time for the supporting and smaller roles, which is why her notes are so important. The casting director will have to rely on memory, past lists and submissions. A casting director keeps track of every audition for every project and takes notes on everyone she sees. In other words, this year's lists are really compilations of last year's notes. Did you read well, even if you didn't book the job?

If you're in a casting director's mental Rolodex, and you're right for a role she is casting, you'll be brought in to pre-read for a specific role or project. Do well, and the casting director will bring you in for a callback with the producers.

STAGE VS. SCREEN

A word here about the difference between the theatre and film/television, also known as New York versus Hollywood. Jerome Robbins, the director of the Broadway musicals *Fiddler on the Roof* and *West Side Story,* spent a full year casting both shows. *West Side,* in particular, required many boys with singing and dancing skills who were too young to have any real stage experience at all. Larry Kert, for example, who became famous as the original Tony and subsequently had a long and distinguished career as a Broadway musical comedy lead, went through numerous auditions which he thought were for one of the Jets. It wasn't until they finally called him to say you're in, that he was told he had been chosen as the lead! Theatre directors tend to sit out there for days and weeks, even months, looking at everyone who comes in, including the notorious "cattle call," or open auditions. Casting directors help them in their hunt, and do the organizational and administrative work, but almost anyone can get seen by the director for a theatre project.

For regional theatres, on the other hand, a dozen productions (each with its own director) may share one casting director in New York who does nearly all the preliminary casting. A pool of actors will then be offered to the directors to choose from.

In Hollywood, there just isn't time—or, frankly, interest—for the producers and directors to sit through all those auditions, so your first audition will probably be for a casting director or casting associate.

THE WRITER

The writer is easily spotted as the worst-dressed person in the room, because he or she spends most days and nights locked in a room either alone or, in the case of a sitcom, rewriting with a dozen other people. If you are auditioning for a sitcom, the head writer will probably be in charge. He or she will have the title of "Executive Producer," will be known in the business as a Show Runner, and will certainly have a very strong say in casting. There are sometimes several executive producers. For feature films and TV movies, writers run the gamut from also being the producer to not being invited to auditions at all. We'll talk more about this later, but this much ought to be common sense: They're not going to appreciate alterations to their dialogue.

THE PRODUCER

It might be useful to know that for the producer, this is probably the most exciting time yet on the project. Suddenly, after weeks, months or years of development, they're actually moving forward. They're in pre-production. *You* are making this possible. *You* are embodying for them what has until now been something of a dream.

In films, many producers will leave casting, especially preliminary auditions, to their directors. In television it is often the other way around. Some producers will micro-manage the casting. And on some projects there will be multiple producers, all putting in their two cents. It's often easier to read for a large group than one person, because it's closer to an "audience" than an "interview." Don't let the number of people sitting behind the table intimidate you. You're a good actor. The larger the audience, the more fun the reading.

The producer, too, is worried about how he is perceived in doing his job, because, depending upon the level of the audition, executives from the network or studio may be looking over his shoulder. And he has a lot on his mind. Casting is only part of it. He is organizing the entire shoot, working on a budget, hiring designers and crew, and hand-holding a star.

THE DIRECTOR

The director will have his own preconception of the role. How close his idea of the role is to the casting director's depends upon their communication. Unfortunately, it sometimes takes a few days of casting—with the director, producer and casting director all talking about the roles and the actors they've seen read—before the casting director truly understands what the producer and director are looking for. And sometimes, before even they understand what they want. Throughout this process, the casting director will revise her thinking and add or subtract actors from upcoming auditions.

Although casting directors may direct you in a reading, the director will often give you a few indications of how he wants you to play the part. (Don't disagree with them. It's just an audition. They want to know if you can "take direction." More about this in Chapter 11.)

Sometimes the producer and the director will disagree on actors, or how a part should be played. The casting director will have to find someone who can please them both.

Remember that the director is human too. While you're checking in with your agent about your next audition, he's checking in with his agent about his next job. Unless he has final cut in his contract—something only a tiny handful of directors do—he's also concerned about the people sitting next to him...

THE EXECUTIVES

This is a breed of men and women attempting the almost impossible task of organizing art as if it were a business. If they're sitting in on your audition, it's good news, because you're probably pretty close to getting the role. It's usually their job to "approve" of the producer's and director's final choices. They mulled over the A-list closely. ("His last picture flopped, cross him off. Her audience won't come to this film, cross her off.") Now they've got to approve of you. Although casting isn't really a cornerstone of their job, in certain situations—television series for example—they're absolutely crucial to your acceptance. They're hoping for some real charisma from the actors to help a project get on its feet, and they're matching your type with the perceived tastes of the demographic audience they want.

In the theatre, there is no such animal, though these days there are multiple producers on a single play or musical. You might even see a few investors out there in the plush seats.

You could be auditioning in any number of situations, from a small office to a large theatre, for any number of people connected with the project. Don't worry about who's on the other side of the table or out there in the dark. Just be polite to all of them. Remember, the guy who went for the coffee today may be directing next season.

That may be a cliché—it's also very true in the entertainment business—but there is more to this advice than the old aphorism, "be careful who you stab on your way up, because you'll meet them on the way down." What you need for a good reading is a pleasant, encouraging atmosphere. *You won't always get it from them.* Maybe they've just been told their budget is cut in half. Maybe Tom Cruise just turned them down. Maybe they're just having a bad day. Bring your own good karma with you!

In Short...

- Don't deal with agencies that are not franchised by an actor's union.

- Don't piss off the assistant. Today's assistants are tomorrow's agents.

- Don't pay for access to agents or casting directors; do pay for classes that teach you something.

. . . .

- Do invite agents to see your work.
- Do short films, student films, plays.
- Do take classes regularly.

2

How You Get an Audition in the First Place

When a project begins casting, the first thing to happen is that a "breakdown" goes out to talent agencies. This is almost always done through the eponymously titled company Breakdown Services, which faxes, emails and/or messengers a copy of the casting director's description of the available roles to all SAG, AFTRA and Equity franchised agents. The agent mails or messengers submissions back to the casting director ASAP.

The digital revolution is gradually changing the nature of how the casting director disseminates this information, and how the agent responds. Neither email nor attempts to create a central on-line Internet database, however, have replaced the traditional use of expensive messenger services. The poor quality of many electronically transmitted photos has been a big reason for this digital stall. Nevertheless, progress dictates the gradual increase in computer-to-computer transfer of breakdowns and submissions in the next decade.

As you know from the previous chapter, by the time you hear about an audition, the casting director has already started making lists of well-known actors she wants to consider. Probably the

assistant has already started calling agencies to check "availabili-ties," that is, to find out if the actors already on the list are:
1) Available for those dates,
2) Interested in the project,
3) Willing to meet or audition, and
4) Able to work within the budget.

These are, in fact, very tricky questions that receive only ten-tative and incomplete answers anyway, because:
1) Availability depends on shooting schedules, which are still tentative at this stage, and always changing.
2) Of course the actor is interested. It's work. But there are actors who claim they "don't do television," others who are only looking for a certain type of project—studio (big money) or independent (good role)—and others who "won't do nudity."
3) Actors, unless they are truly unavailable, are almost always willing to meet or audition, though sometimes only if they like the script, and sometimes only if there's an offer on the table.
4) What an actor gets paid is not always dependent on his quote. Sylvester Stallone got $20 million to make a picture, yet he took a role in *Cop Land* (he was brilliant), and that film's entire budget was only $15 million.

But "availabilities" don't really matter to you. What matters is what it says on the breakdown, so let's get to it. Here are two examples:

(File 0320p05-ia) L
Original (File 0225p05-ia) L

DELIVERED IN LA Monday, March 24, 1997:

"SEX AND THE CITY"
1/2 HOUR PILOT / HBO
DRAFT: FEB. 4, 1997

Exec. Producer: Darren Star
Director: Susan Seidelman
Writer: Darren Star
Casting Directors: Ellie Kanner / Russell Gray
New York Casting Directors: Billy Hopkins / Kerry Barden
Start Date: End of April
Location: **NEW YORK**

WRITTEN SUBMISSIONS ONLY TO:

ELLIE KANNER / RUSSELL GRAY
20TH CENTURY FOX
10201 W. PICO BLVD.
BUILDING 777
L.A. CA 90035

[SAMANTHA] **Mid 30s**, one of Carrie's best friends, Samantha is a self-possessed young woman, a successful New York working woman with her own business who tells her girlfriends, "Look, for the first time in Manhattan history, we have as much money and power as men. With the equal luxury of treating men like sex objects." Convinced that "the 'right guy' is an illusion" and that women can and should have unemotional sexual encounters as often as they like, Samantha is blessed (or deluded) with an abundance of self-confidence...SERIES REGULAR (10) *(Copyright 2003, BREAKDOWN SERVICES, LTD.)*

[STANFORD BLATCH] **In his mid to late 30s** and gay, he is one of Carrie's closest friends. He's the owner of a talent agency who, at the moment, is down to a single client -- an underwear model. A passionate person, somewhat high-strung, Stanford is horrified as he watches Carrie put the moves on an old boyfriend who's dumped her many times in the past. He reminds Carrie, "I don't have time to clean up this mess for the fourth time."...SERIES REGULAR (13)

[MIRANDA HOBBES] In her **mid 30s**, tall, thin and pseudo-attractive, she bemoans the state of love and relationships today. Somewhat cynical, Miranda feels that by the time you get to your mid 30s why should you settle. Miranda has pretty much "decided that all men are a--holes." She goes out on a date with the very nice Skipper Johnson, and even though she thinks he's too nice, she's willing to over look that one "flaw," for a night of passion...SERIES REGULAR (7)

[MR. BIG] A very handsome man in his **early 40s**, a cigar smoker, he is "like the next Donald Trump. But single, younger and better looking." Eligible and wealthy, as well as charming, he is nonplussed by Carrie's statement about men feeling nothing after having sex. He's quick to point out that obviously she's never been in love...RECURRING (22)

[SKIPPER JOHNSON] **26 years old**, a website creator, Skipper is a helpless romantic who believes that "love conquers all." Convinced that what's missing in Manhattan is the "space for romance," Skipper tells Carrie that he's a sensitive man who doesn't objectify women. He's delighted when Carrie sets him up with Miranda and is immediately smitten by her..RECURRING (8) *(Copyright 2003, BREAKDOWN SERVICES, LTD.)*

[CAPOTE DUNCAN] **Mid to late 30s**, handsome and preppy, he is a Sr. V.P. at Simon and Schuster, also an investment banker at Goldman Sachs, and "one of the city's most notoriously ungettable bachelors." A real cad, he spends an evening with one woman, then tells her he's heading out to a singles bar because, as he puts it, "I need to have sex tonight."...RECURRING (7) *(Copyright 2003, BREAKDOWN SERVICES, LTD.)*

STORY LINE: CARRIE BRADSHAW, a columnist for the "New York Herald," chronicles the demise of romance in Manhattan...

(File 0710f07-lk) L
(O. 0623f02-ia) L
THE PLAYTONE COMPANY
LIONS GATE / GOLD CIRCLE FILMS
"MY BIG FAT GREEK WEDDING"
FEATURE FILM
DRAFT: 6/22/00

DEL'D IN LA Wed., July 12, 2000, Vol. 2000, #0712
Producers: Tom Hanks, Gary Goetzman, Rita Wilson
Director: Joel Zwick
Writer: Nia Vardalos
Casting Directors: Meg Liberman / Cami Patton
Casting Associate: Lisa Ystrom
Casting Assistant: Marilyn Pinzur
Start Date: Approx. 9/5/2000
Location: Toronto

WRITTEN SUBMISSIONS ONLY TO:

LIBERMAN / PATTON CASTING
4311 WILSHIRE BLVD.
SUITE 606
LOS ANGELES, CA 90010

Use THE LINK/STARCASTER to submit actors immediately for this project.

TOULA PORTOKALOS: CAST (NIA VARDALOS)

PLEASE NOTE: This is a Greek comedy. Please submit actors who can play believeable Greeks and actors who have comic timing. Please submit both name and non-name actors for the leads.

MANAGERS: PLEASE DON'T DOUBLE SUBMIT.

[IAN MILLER]   **THIS IS THE ONE CHARACTER WHO ISN'T GREEK.** In his early 30s, handsome, WASPy and charming in that dorky-guy-next-door way, he is an English teacher at a local high school, a laid-back, easily likable fellow, with a gentle, unflappable manner. Very much attracted to Toula (and vice versa), he is very accepting of her raucous and often overbearing Greek family, actually delighted by the show of enthusiasm and "personality" evidenced by her relatives. As he tells Toula, "Who cares if you have a weird family, who doesn't? I want to spend time with you." Soon after, he asks Toula to marry him, unperturbed by the idea that he will have to be baptized in the Greek Orthodox Church before tying the knot. Ian is refreshingly straightforward, and assures a very worried Toula that whatever happens he can handle it…LEAD (20)

[GUS PORTOKALOS]   Toula's father, seen from 40 to 60, he is an amiable, goofy, hard-working Greek immigrant who's always putting his foot in his mouth. Gus is very much a traditionalist, proud of his Greek heritage, and equally proud of the fact that he came to this country with only 8 dollars in his pocket, but with hard work and perseverance was able to found a thriving business. Clearly eager to see Toula married, he is distraught when she intimates that she would like to go to college. Upset because he thinks she wants to abandon the family, he is taken aback when he learns that she is dating a non-Greek fellow. However, his blustering distrust of this "xeno" (foreigner), eventually gives way to respect and admiration.…LEAD (1)

[MARIA PORTOKALOS]   Seen from her mid 30s to 60, she is Toula's mother, a very traditional Greek wife and matriarch. Bright and determined, possessed of an awareness not shared by her husband, she knows that her daughter Toula is not happy and that her desires to go to college are an expression of a "spirit," Fully aware that while the man may be the head of the house, but the wife is the neck (where the neck turns the head follows), Maria promises Toula that she will intercede on her behalf. Later, when Gus laments the fact that his daughter is going to marry a non-Greek, she softly reminds him that the two young people love one another…LEAD (3)

[NIKKI]   In her early to mid 30s, Toula's cousin, Nikki is also Greek, married to a Greek man. She is "boobs galore, blood-red fake nails and teased enormous Jackie-O-on-crack hairdo." She's flamboyant, loud, well-meaning and larger than life. Never subtle, Nikki is a life-force, and takes it upon herself to handle much of the wedding arrangements, including the hideous turquoise bridesmaid gowns…LEAD (14)

[AUNT VOULA]   Seen from her late 40s to early 60s, she is Maria's younger sister, Toula's aunt. Also Greek, she is an effusive, good-hearted, opinionated woman, clearly devoted to her family. She proudly shows the new in-laws through her sister's garish home, oblivious to its tackiness…LEAD (9)

BREAKDOWN SERVICES, LTD.   Los Angeles   New York   Vancouver   London
BREAKDOWN SERVICES, LTD.   (310) 276-9166   (212) 869-2003   (604) 943-7100   (01) 459-2781
BREAKDOWN SERVICES, LTD.
BREAKDOWN SERVICES, LTD.
www.breakdownservices.com   The Link: www.submitlink.com

THE PLAYTONE COMPANY
LIONS GATE / GOLD CIRCLE FILMS
"MY BIG FAT GREEK WEDDING"
FEATURE FILM   PAGE TWO...

[NICK POROTKALOS]   Seen from 19-31, he is Toula's younger brother, a hairy and stocky fellow with a playful nature and a good heart. He is perhaps not the brightest kid on the block. The cook at Dancing Zorbas (the Greek restaurant owned by his family), Nick is also a promising artist, always designing new jacket covers for the menus. At first he does not understand his sister's need for independence and asks her in confidence if she went to college because she hated the family. However, later, he comes to understand that what she did by trying to live her own life was an act of bravery. In fact, Nick has decided that he, too, would like to go to college, but says he'll start slow, just a few night courses in painting and art...LEAD (10)

[YIAYIA]   She is Gus' mother, an elderly Greek woman. Plays 60-80. She's under five feet tall, dressed completely in black and has a face like an apple carving. She's senile and doesn't know what's going on. But she can take care of herself; she's not pathetic. She's also convinced that Turks are still after her. Actress must be healthy and vital...

[HILLARY & RODNEY MILLER]   Ian's WASPy parents, they are in their late 50s, refined, trim and cultivated. They live in a townhouse decorated in muted tones. Gracious, but icy, and extremely polite, they welcome Toula to their home, but grow increasingly unnerved by references to her family. Later, when they meet the Portokalos clan, it's evident they feel smothered, not sure how to react. But by the time of the wedding, while the Millers are still reserved, they've clearly happily accepted their new and very colorful Greek in-laws...

[ATHENA]   In her 30s, (ages from 19 to 35), she is Toula's older sister, already married with three screaming boys and a baby on the way. Seen wearing her ever-present frilly homemaker's apron, she chatters happily to her mother about the many chores she's got planned for the day. Clearly, Athena is delighted with her lot in life ...

[UNCLE TAKI]   Late 40s to early 60s, he is Aunt Voula's husband, under the thumb of his opinionated wife. A thoughtful sort, not the type who reacts in haste, he tries to tell Gus that Toula (who's still unmarried and in college) seems to be "okay with her life."...

[ANGELO]   In his early 30s, he is Nikki's brother. Angelo is truly gorgeous and wears a silk shirt open to reveal his welcome mat of furry chest. He and Nikki (with whom he is always arguing) run a dry cleaning establishment...

[MIKE]   A pleasant fellow, he is Ian's friend and colleague. He only laughs when Ian tells him that Toula has a lot of cousins if he's interested in a date...

[PRIEST]   60s+. A good friend of the family, this Greek Orthodox Priest is only too happy to marry Toula and Ian, provided Ian is baptized into the church. Somewhat forward thinking, he reminds Gus that "It's one thing to preserve traditions. It's another thing to live in the past." Of course, he will, nonetheless, be performing the ceremony in Greek...

[MRS. WHITE]   Age? It's hard to tell. She is the neighborhood gossip, wearing curlers, fuzzy slippers, cigarette in one hand, lime rickey in the other...2 speeches, 2 scenes (7)

[GIRL]   She is a pretty, fair-haired little girl, a Brownie...2 lines, 1 scene (2)

[TEACHER]   He/she is the teacher at Greek school, teaching the children their native tongue...1 line in Greek, 1 scene (2)

[ATHENA AT 15]   This is Toula's older, "perfect" sister...no lines, 1 line, (4)

[ATHENA AT 19]   This is Athena at 19, still "a major brown noser."...no lines, 1 scene (8)

[TOULA AT 12]   This is Toula at 12, a chubby, observant, rather unhappy youngster who likes to think of herself as an American...1 line, 3 scenes (4)

BREAKDOWN SERVICES, LTD.
BREAKDOWN SERVICES, LTD.
BREAKDOWN SERVICES, LTD.
BREAKDOWN SERVICES, LTD.
www.breakdownservices.com   The Link: www.submitlink.com

Los Angeles   New York   Vancouver   London
(310) 276-9166 (212) 869-2003 (604) 943-7100 (01) 459-2781

THE PLAYTONE COMPANY
LIONS GATE / GOLD CIRCLE FILMS
"MY BIG FAT GREEK WEDDING"
FEATURE FILM   PAGE THREE...

[TOULA AT 16-20]   At 16, Toula is still fat, now working at her dad's restaurant ...1 line, 2 scenes (8)

[NICK AT 11]   This is Nick at 11, seen eating breakfast with his family...no lines, 1 scene (4)

[NICK AT 15]   Nick at 15 is "the hairiest Greek in Chicago."...no lines, 1 scene (8)

[YIANNI]   Athena's husband, he is "a shepherd" from Gus's village...1 line, 4 scenes (8)

[AUNT FRIEDA]   She is one of Toula's aunts, gold-toothed, effusive and somewhat overbearing, but clearly well-meaning...2 lines, 3 scenes (63)

[FRIEND #1]   A friend of Toula, around 12, she/he is a precocious kid with attitude...1 line, 1 scene (5)

[NANCY LAUDER]   An absolutely beautiful woman, she pretends to be a music teacher when she asks Ian directions to the office. However, we soon discover she's a stripper, hired by Nick and Angelo...1 speech & 2 lines, 1 scene (80)

[AUNT NOTA]   She is one of Toula's aunts. She has come all the way from Canada for the wedding...1 line, 1 scene (88)

[AUNT LEXY]   A loud and cheerful woman, she is another of Toula's aunts...1 speech & 2 lines, 2 scenes (96)

[COUSIN JENNIE]   This eager cousin of Toula's arrives with some concealer when Toula wakes up on the morning of her wedding with a huge pimple on her face...2 lines, 2 scenes (96)

[COUSIN MARIANTHI]   This cousin, a bridesmaid with an iron burn on her gown, snippily asks Nick about the other limos...1 line, 2 scenes (100)

[PARIS]   This is Toula's 6 year old daughter, a chubby, knock-kneed, glasses-wearing dork...1 line, 1 scene (109)

STORY LINE: Toula Porotokalos has always had a difficult time accepting her Greek roots, often embarrassed as a child by her overbearing, raucous and loud, but still loving and well-meaning family. When she meets and falls in love with very WASPy IAN MILLER, she's not sure how he'll react to her weird relatives, delighted when he actually embraces them, seemingly delighted by her family's exuberance and zest for life....

Having received a breakdown, an agent will immediately pull the pictures and résumés of the actors on his client list who he thinks are appropriate for each role and zoom them over to the casting director.

"Why wasn't I submitted for that?"

A good question, unless you're the agent who has to answer it. Agents make judgement calls on their own clients every day. They go by the breakdowns initially, but after reading the script and discussing it with the casting director, may discover that some roles have already changed. The agent will usually err on the side of more submissions rather than fewer, because they know the casting director will cull the list anyway. If you hear about a role you think you'd be right for, don't hesitate to call your agent and say so. There's a chance he doesn't know about it. There's a chance he didn't think of you. Be prepared, however, to hear, "I did submit you. They didn't want to see you." Agents don't call with bad news if they can help it. They'd rather not call at all.

Some roles won't be open to auditions because they are reserved for actors with a certain level of profile, or TVQ (a talent likability rating favored by TV producers). This happens not only at the obvious, celebrity/star level, but often for good character roles as well. Harvey Keitel, whom the average teenage moviegoer has probably never heard of, means something on the festival circuit. Celebrity guest stars on television series can boost ratings. Often a casting director will pursue a celebrity and read lesser known actors at the same time as a back-up.

A casting director may know that a certain role could be demanding, and eliminate a submission because she doesn't see enough significant credits. Other times she may just feel the actor's "look"—the headshot being all she has to go on—isn't right. Occasionally a casting director may know the actor's work well enough to make a decision without pre-reading him or her. Most casting directors won't eliminate an actor who has a bad reputation, because that's a very subjective call, and it's too early in the process. They will, however, warn the director or producer if an actor has a history of being "difficult," because if she didn't reveal this and an actor became a nightmare to work with, the casting director would be blamed.

"Suppose I don't have an agent.
How can I get submitted for a role?"

There's no harm in submitting yourself. Mail your picture and résumé to the casting director. It is no longer possible to "drop by" a casting office, even to leave a picture and résumé with the assistant. Office buildings and studio lots are too carefully guarded in our post 9/11 world. Attach a short note—no longer than a brief paragraph—saying you heard about the role and would like an audition. Most casting directors are very conscientious about opening all submissions, since, unlike scripts, there is no legal danger in looking at an unsolicited picture and résumé. Also, you can ask for a general interview. If you're new in town, there's no harm in canvassing all the casting directors to let them know you're here and ready for your big break. If you do ask for an audition, don't expect to get one immediately. Keep in mind that casting directors need to see the new crop of actors every season. Casting directors worry about overlooking a new face that could get hot quickly. However, don't badger the office. There's a very fine line between being persistent and being obnoxious.

Don't send your demo reel unless it's requested, and don't use the fax machine for pictures and résumés. A résumé alone doesn't do much for an actor, and photographs look pretty bad unless the machine is capable of handling halftones. Anyway, casting directors need their fax machines for too many other chores, and it's usually standing all too close to the trash basket.

Now, how about that picture and résumé of yours?

In Short...

- Don't be a pest.

. . . .

- Do stay in touch with your agent.
- Do submit your picture/résumé to casting directors every three to six months.

3

Pictures, Résumés and Demo Reels

Your picture/résumé is your calling card. You're going to leave copies all over the place. (That is, you're going to leave them in casting offices. One actor, working as a valet at an industry restaurant, left his résumé on the front seat of every black Mercedes. Not recommended.)

This document has two sides, but the picture is the first thing casting people look at, so let's consider it the "front," and start there.

YOUR PICTURE

It's pretty standard: a headshot. Photography ranges from the kind of thing that gets taken when you're booked for a felony, to seductive, soft-focus, full-color *Vogue* stuff. The former is probably not a good idea unless you're going to specialize in psychopaths. The latter isn't such a good idea either. The more "glamorous" the picture, the less realistic it looks. We know we can make you look glamorous. What the casting people need to see is *you*. The dramatic shadows of film noir are great, but limiting. We're more likely to think highly of the photographer than the subject. One very realistic headshot that shows *you* to your best advantage is perfect. Don't go for full body shots unless you're a model—they're not necessary for actors.

Okay, what *is* your advantage? If you're a well-above-average looking woman, are you going to show bare shoulders? Cleavage? We're not in a position to tell you no. Certainly most female casting in television and film is about sex appeal. If you got it, flaunt it. But don't go overboard. If your cleavage is the focal point of the picture, we're probably going to think "cheap," more than "good actor." This goes for men, too. The open shirt and bulging pecs make a statement. Is it what you want us to know about you? Is that the focus of the picture?

Basically, there are two simple criteria:

1) Realistic. The casting director wants to believe that if you walk in, she's not going to say, "Who's this?" (You won't believe how many times we hear, "She doesn't look anything like her picture," at auditions.)

2) Flattering. Give it your best shot.

So, realistic and flattering. Do these two issues conflict? Not if you're honest. Get some help with honesty. Show them to your friends, your family. See what your photographer thinks of the various poses. But in the end, you've got to be happy.

If we had to describe the best headshots, we'd probably say that they "jump out" at you. The face is arresting, the expression is interesting, the lighting, clothes and background are supportive, not intrusive. And, most of all, perhaps, you look like *you've got something going on behind the eyes.* Unless you're going to specialize in dim-witted bimbos. Well, even then. A good headshot stands not just for who you are, but indicates *how well you can act.* Impossible, of course. Ridiculous, yes. But some people "photograph well," and some don't. And what "photogenic" really means is, we can read character in your face. After all, when Clint Eastwood raises his eyebrow, he says it all with just a look.

As with your in-person auditions, sincerity is the key. Get a shot that doesn't look overly posed, one in which you look natural—no matter how much effort it takes.

Photos taken with a disposable camera or an indoor photo taken with a single flash source aren't going to be good enough. They're almost guaranteed to be unflattering; it's amazing how a single light source can flatten your features. But it's also something worse: amateurish. It's a giveaway that your dad took the photo. Go to a professional photographer for a sitting, even if your dad *is* a professional photographer. You need an unbiased opinion to help you make your ultimate decision. You needn't spend a lot of money. A good photographer can capture many moods in a single session. Some pointers:

- Looking for a photographer? Ask around. Look at the head-shots of actor acquaintances. Look at the photographer's portfolio. If the photographer has a unique, individual and specific style, then that's probably what he's going to make you look like. Is it really you? Try to find a photographer who is flexible. Your headshot probably shouldn't resemble *Vogue* or *Rolling Stone* photography. While a good head-shot is dramatic, the drama shouldn't be the prime focus. You should. Again, a picture that is too perfect is suspicious. ("You think she really looks like that?") As is a picture that isn't professional. ("Has he done any work at all?")

- Smile or not? No perfect answer. Many actors have one of each, and send the smile for the comedy, the serious for the drama. This can get tricky, what with all the "dramedies" out there these days. It really depends on which flatters you the most. Great teeth? Let's see them. Ingenuous, sincere look while smiling? Very good—sincerity is a key. But a really big smile tends to limit the range of emotions we can imagine. The great Russian film director Eisenstein once showed an audience film of a horrible accident, then cut to a reaction shot. Next he showed the audience film of a cute, newborn baby, then cut to a reaction shot. The audience judged the actor as reacting to both circumstances brilliantly, only to be told that Eisenstein had intercut *the same reaction shot* in both sequences. In other words, viewers can read a lot into an expression, provided it's not overly specific. Don't limit our imagination too much.

- Many actors carry several versions, which might include "lead" and "character actor" in addition to smiling and serious. Just be careful not to use that evil grin with the Max Factor scar if you're up for a romantic lead. Know who you are—a lead or a character actor, an ingenue or a mom—and have the appropriate pictures to support that type.

- The paper your picture is printed on will effect your picture. Lithograph, glossy and pearltone are three available finishes, with glossy being standard for a long time.
- Border or borderless? Tilted frame or straight? Doesn't really matter, but why waste that space? Personally, we think a borderless, straightforward picture reads a little better, perhaps because the white frame shouts "headshot!" and reminds us that it's only a picture. (Not to draw too much out of this, but let's remember that even still photography is there to suck us in, to get us to *suspend our disbelief,* just as for a drama. A border can prompt us to remember that it's just a picture.)
- How close is too close? Herbert Brodkin was the director of photography on a 1960s television series called *The Defenders.* He invented the ECU, film school tech talk for an extreme close-up, otherwise known as "the Brodkin." We have him to thank for the macro-photography of actors and actresses faces. It's a striking look, virtually eliminating anything that could distract from the expression, including hair. But it's not a good idea as a headshot. Don't use a close-up so tight that we can't quite tell what you look like. That goes for an extreme profile, too. It's not enough of your face. We need to see all of you, including your hair. (Which shouldn't cover half your face.)
- How much of an angle? Whatever works for you. It's usually best to look at us (the camera) rather than moodily off into the distance. Be careful, however, of absolutely straight on. It's a little too "mug shot," and tends to flatten faces. Most photographers will want a little angle, or the picture will be too bland. Even if you're only slightly turned, you're going to want to choose your best side. Let the photographer help you with that. Get some poses of both sides to compare. Photographers should offer plenty of shots at one "sitting," then give you the proofs to choose from.
- Don't wear clothes that distract from your face. Wear simple colors with a neckline that suits you. Something that works in black and white. Bring several variations of wardrobe to the shoot—formal, informal, various necklines—and see what works best.

- Don't wear any jewelry that distracts from your face. Why give Cartier publicity when it's your face you're selling? That single gold stud that makes a man look macho limits your character range. Those dangling plastic saucers aren't going to increase a woman's sex appeal in a picture. It's all right to wear a tasteful little something if you think it gives you character, or supports who you are, but in general, in the "who you are" category, you'll want to leave as much leeway as possible.

- Indoors or out? If you can come up with a good shot of yourself standing in front of the Grand Canyon, great. Send it to the grandparents. Anything that distracts from your face shouldn't be in the picture. This is not to say that we haven't seen some terrific pictures that happen to have been taken outdoors, but photographers can direct their lighting better indoors—the sun takes too much equipment to control—and backgrounds should be fairly neutral, so they don't distract from *you*.

- One shot or four? Four 4" by 5" pictures in a composite gives you four different moods and expressions, but generally for film and television you should have at least one full size picture. Again, however, different opportunities present different needs. Character actors who have played a variety of roles may benefit from showing their range, and commercial actors usually have composites to show variety. In general, one good headshot is all you need to begin with.

- If you're the girl-next-door type, don't get all dolled up and take a picture that looks like Cher on stage. Casting directors get a little miffed when you turn out to be a completely different type than the one they saw in the picture. And don't hand out pictures that no longer look like you. Casting people just hate it when they call in someone who looks 20 years old in their picture and a 45-year-old shows up. Men need to remember this too.

- Don't let your pictures get out of date. If you've cut off your hair, you'll need a new picture. If you've grown a beard or shaved one off, you'll need a new picture. If you're five years older and still using the same headshot, see paragraph above.

- Don't print your agency logo on your picture, unless they're going to pay for it. You'll just have to purchase new pictures if you change agencies. The agency logo will be on your résumé.
- You should, however, print *your name* on the picture. It connects the name and the face, and frankly, it's convenient for casting people. They don't want to have to turn it over just to identify you. Sometimes pictures and résumés come apart. If that happens and your name is not on the picture, it goes into the trash.
- Color or black and white? Black and white is traditional and still holds a near monopoly, color almost unheard of before the new age of home technology, except for high-fashion models. It's a growing idea, however, and we'd bet that in a decade or two color will be more popular, as the dissemination of pictures becomes more Internet and email driven. Not to say that black and white will ever go away. Look at fashion magazines, which still feature a lot of black-and-white photography. There's something very seductive about black and white. At this point we'd say you probably want to take some in black and white and a few in color, and keep the color handy for special circumstances. Redheads are the exception to this rule and should always have a good color headshot. If it's too expensive, make sure to note it on your résumé—in fact, note red hair on your résumé no matter what. As long as there is still a big difference in cost of duplication, however, don't sweat it. After all, let's discount the idea that a picture is going to get you a job right now. It's not. It's just to help get your foot in the door.

> • • •
>
> Harpo's famous wig was red in vaudeville. When the Marx Brothers began to make motion pictures, it was changed to blond, because red didn't work in the black-and-white photography of the day.
>
> • • •

- Don't use the Doris Day/soft-focus lens. Your face should be crisp and clear, not shrouded in romantic fog. No harm in covering up a pimple or blemish with makeup or re-touching (an item which used to cost a great deal, but is now simple and inexpensive with digital photography), but keep to the basic *you*.

- Don't use that great publicity shot of you as Richard III, complete with humpback and club foot. The headshot is not a chance to show them your range of roles. Theatre people don't care about your picture. They use it only to remember your on-stage audition after you've gone. Film and television people are more attuned to your picture, because of the medium. They want accuracy.

- You're going to need plenty of copies of your headshot, and unless you have pretty sophisticated computer equipment and either a scanned photo or a digital photo to begin with, you'll want them made at a commercial photo lab. Since even one 8" by 10" can cost a fair amount these days, you'll generally want to order in bulk to save money. We'd say not more than 100, which should give you a good reduction in price. More than that and even you are going to get tired of the shot. It used to be that a full size negative had to be made—that's the expensive part—and then dupes could be run off cheaply. You had the negative, and could re-order without that expense. Now a lot of professional photographers are using digital, which has an enormous advantage in that you can see the results right then and there, and should be less expensive to duplicate. Ask around and compare prices. Contemporary costs are easy to judge by the advertisements you see in the trade papers.

- Don't go to a photographer who an agent or casting director insists upon. That spells kickback. Recommendations, sure. But if a job or representation ever depends upon your paying a friend of theirs, you're one step away from the casting couch. That's not to say the photographer might not be terrific, but why chance it? Do your own research. Look at photographer's portfolios, talk to other actors about their experiences, compare prices and make your own decision.

This is a very subjective area, but a few examples might help you decide on what you'll want...

A great beauty. The lighting is just dramatic enough to accentuate the face and not hide it.

This tells you a lot about the actor's natural ebullience and the picture radiates charm. It works even though it shows more than just his face. Hey, there are exceptions to every rule...

A strong headshot (though today we'd probably say "lose the moustache").

*A composite for a character actor with a very wide range.
Unnecessary unless you're at least 50 with as many credits
behind you. Composites are only for commercial submissions;
they are not to be used for film and television.*

IVANA MILICEVIC

Here are two additional headshots of contemporary working actors.

GREG SERANO

YOUR RÉSUMÉ

On the "back," then, is your résumé. This information is more important than you might think. A résumé with significant credits—by which we mean a certain amount of past work for your age, at a fairly high level of the profession—certainly gives casting people reassurance. A "hit" in your past can really make them sit up and take notice. Everyone wants to associate themselves with success. But new faces are always sought after too, so don't be embarrassed if you have only a few credits. (Hollywood is more often enamored with new faces than it is with the same old faces it already knows.) If you're 21 years old and you've done a dozen classic roles in college, what the heck, at the very least, we know you're dedicated.

Just to tell you how lucky you are to be living in the computer age: When we first went into the business, there were no "personal" computers. To look good, a résumé had to be "typeset" and then 100 copies printed out. Less than a hundred was hardly economical. When, after passing out a dozen of them, you got a job, you had to go back and pay to have the whole thing done again, adding your most recent credit. Today, you can keep your résumé on your computer. Print out a couple of copies when you're on your way to a job. Update it as often as you want. Play with the format. For theatre auditions, place your theatre credits on top. For films, film. For television, television. Worried that because you've done too many musicals, the Rep company won't take you seriously? Cut the musicals and emphasize the Shakespeare. Always have a couple of hard copies ready. Don't rely on your printer to work every time you get a last minute call from your agent. Bring a hard copy (attached to your headshot) with you to every audition, whether or not you know your agent has sent one in advance.

What's on it, of course, is the real issue.

YOUR NAME

Your stage name, exactly as listed in SAG, AFTRA or Equity. Not your real name, though these days we think most actors retain their real names. But consider: Would Tony Curtis be as handsome as Bernard Schwartz? Would Marilyn Monroe be as sexy as Norma

Jean Baker? Would Mel Brooks be as funny as Melvin Kaminsky? (Well, yes to that last one, anyway.)

YOUR AGENT'S NAME, ADDRESS AND PHONE NUMBER

If you don't have an agent yet, list your own pager or cell phone, or a phone number that has voice mail or an answering machine.

Actors, and especially actresses, are generally warned not to give out their home phone numbers, and certainly not their addresses. Too many wackos out there. Message machines, at least, allow you to screen your calls. (*69 allows you to call back instantly, which is none too soon for actors "waiting to hear.") Cell phones are good, because they don't give away your address, and you can keep them handy. One way or another, you have to follow our one most basic rule: Don't be out of touch. Actors and actresses should have pagers, cell phones—anything that allows you to be reached almost instantly. If you change numbers, be sure to have a referral on your old one for several months.

YOUR UNION AFFILIATIONS

If you're in a union, put it on your resume. SAG, AFTRA, Equity—whatever you belong to. It says you're professional. But don't lie; it's too easy to get caught (casting directors will know by the credits).

• • •

I was casting a pilot and we were down to the wire. We had a table reading on Monday and were testing at the network for one of the lead roles the Saturday before. Business Affairs had been negotiating with an agent who represented one of our top choices and it was not going well. As of Friday evening the agent passed on behalf of the client. On Saturday morning Business Affairs decided to cave in and give the agent what he wanted for his client. The agent tried desperately to get in touch with the client, to no avail. The actress didn't have a pager or cell phone, and went out for the day without checking her messages. The agent couldn't reach the client and we had to move forward and make a decision so we would have our lead actress cast and at the table read. This actress missed an opportunity to become a series regular on a show that lasted several years because she didn't check her messages.

—E.K.

• • •

YOUR VITAL STATISTICS

Height and weight—no point in fibbing here. Hair and eye color used to be common, but they're pretty pointless today. For one thing, your picture is attached, and for another, both are easily changed with Clairol or contacts. No one wants to put down their age—too limiting—so "age range" has evolved. But that's also pretty useless, because any good actor will list a range far greater than any good director would allow. There's just too much talent out there. Directors are looking for an exact match. By the same token, maybe other roles haven't been cast yet. Also, if you really nail the part, maybe they can revise the character to make it more age-appropriate for you. All in all, we'd say that "age range" is unnecessary. Don't limit yourself. Let them do that. (But if you are under 18, say so because it affects your work status.)

YOUR CREDITS

- Categorize your credits. A section on "films," another on "television," and "stage." Most actors put "commercials—list available upon request" if they have done ads, which is probably a good idea. A list of products isn't really going to grab our eye ("Wow, she's done waxy floor build-up!") and they're not considered very relevant to acting (which is unfair, because they can require a lot of skill). We might even suggest that producers and directors don't want actors who have done too many commercials. They might see them as overexposed. (If you're actually up for a commercial, this list—which you should keep current—will be requested, because ad agencies don't want to hire an actor who's been pitching a competitive product.)
- Within each category, put them in reverse chronological order. That is, latest role first, and going backwards to your Lady Macbeth at George Washington Elementary School. You can re-arrange a year or two here and there in order to put a really good credit at the top of the list. Don't list the dates.
- For stage roles, list the name of the role. "Falstaff" in *Henry VI*, for example, tells us something. For film and television, list "Lead," "Featured," "Guest Star," etc. Unless you played

Mr. Belvedere on *Mr. Belvedere*, we're probably not going to remember the character's name. (Okay, what was the family's name? See, you don't remember, either.) We're suspicious whenever we see a title that doesn't list the billing (such as "Lead," "Featured, "Guest Star," etc.) because we think immediately you were just an extra and don't want to say so. (There's nothing wrong with being an extra. Before the Reagan era, they even had their own union. But don't include extra work on your résumé.)

- The credit should include the studio and network. Theatre credits should say "Broadway," "Off-Broadway," "National Tour," or the name of the regional theatre, school, or producing entity, i.e., "State Theatre of Georgia," or "Ensemble Studio Theatre, Buffalo" or "The Goodman, Chicago," whatever identifies the venue.

- List the project's director, if it was a professional engagement. We can't tell you how many résumés we've seen that are skimpy on these details. It doesn't do the least bit of good to put on your résumé something like:

> Theatre:
> Romeo in *Romeo and Juliet*
> Hamlet in *Hamlet*
> Mitch in *A Streetcar Named Desire.*

If the theatre could be anywhere from the Old Vic to non-Equity dinner theatre, we aren't going to be impressed. The fact is, writing "Greensborough North Carolina Summer Musical Theatre" is better than leaving the theatre out altogether. It may not be Broadway, but it sounds real. In Hollywood, a lot of films have awfully generic titles, and if it didn't make *Variety*'s opening weekend list or earn a festival award, it's probably not going to ring a bell. Just adding "Force Ten Productions, directed by Malachi Schmuck, produced by Willy Cheatam" gives it at least a little credence. Casting people will seldom risk showing their ignorance by asking for the details. But be prepared if they do. Don't make it up as you go along.

And if you are seriously being considered, where you played roles and who you worked for become increasingly important. Very often, when casting gets down to the wire, a producer or director will call one of your previous producers or directors and ask for a reference. How was she to work with? Was he difficult? That's one reason for listing them. (If you had a really bad experience with a particular director, consider forgetting to put his name in, or dropping the credit altogether.) Another is that the people you're auditioning for might know the people you worked for, and that can be a nice conversation starter.

• Don't ever, ever lie. And don't fudge either. Don't make it seem as if you had a major role when you had one line. One, you can be caught, and two, you'll spend your whole interview worrying about getting caught.

• Check for mistakes. Don't ever let your agent's assistant type up your résumé without checking it yourself. We once saw this credit listed for a Broadway show:

Fiddler on the Roof—
understudy Tommy

You may not see anything wrong with that, but an experienced casting director will. Tommy? Of Anatevka? There is no "Tommy" in *Fiddler.*

YOUR SPECIAL SKILLS

Look for things that might be interesting to a director. A black belt in martial arts would certainly be useful

---

• • •

Don't lie on your résumé. If you were only an extra or a day player on a particular show, please don't tell me you were "a guest star" or "recurring." I can't tell you how many times I've sat in on auditions and, while glancing at an actor's résumé, realized that the actor lied. How would I know this? Because I had been a writer-producer on whatever show he/she had lied about and *knew* that the actor wasn't a "recurring" anything. And, if you lie once, I have to assume that everything else on your résumé isn't true, either. But—and this is important—there are a lot of other writer-producers who disagree with me on this one. These writer-producers could care less what's on your résumé; they just want to see how you handle this particular audition. So I guess I'll just leave this one up to you.

—Constance Burge
Creator of *Charmed*;
Writer for *Ed, Boston Public,*
Ally McBeal

• • •

these days. Cooking doesn't count, even if you won the bake-off back home. Special skills are things a director would have a tough time teaching in rehearsal. A degree in law or medicine would certainly perk up the eye of *Law and Order* and *ER* people. A Ph.D. in English Lit doesn't matter. If you spent a decade as a policeman or fireman before you tried acting, that's helpful; it means you'll have real credibility in certain roles. Anything that *you* would not need to be trained for that other actors would, is good.

"Dialects" is one of our least favorites. Any good actor should be able to learn an accent if called upon, but don't list it on your résumé unless you can fool a native. Fluency in a foreign language can be eye-catching (especially if they're casting an international thriller), but don't list a language you are not conversationally fluent in. It has happened more than once that a director looked up from seeing "Spanish" on a résumé, and said rapidly, "*Aprendiste Espanol en escuela o en un pais de Sur Americano?*" and the actor went blank.

"Jogging" once appeared on a résumé and made us laugh almost as much as the beauty pageant contestant whose talent was packing a suitcase (see her in the classic cult film *Smile)*. If you play a musical instrument well enough to sight read, that could be good.

The problem with "special skills" is that people who read résumés are very jaded. If it says "horseback riding," they figure, big deal, anyone can ride a horse. Don't put something like that down unless you can also say, "2000 Olympics, USA Equestrian team," which clearly sets you apart as the real thing.

Things like "juggling" are in between. Could be useful, but any actor worth his salt has mastered the three-balls-in-the-air routine. If you're not Cirque du Soleil level, or close to it, it doesn't really matter. Although, if you think you could get even just one audition by listing it, then go ahead.

. . .

A good-looking actress once auditioned for a role as a lifeguard on a *Baywatch* episode. (Wearing an outfit so skin tight the muted discussion behind the table revolved around whether or not she was wearing underwear. But this isn't about her outfit.) When she got the role and reported to the beach, it turned out *she couldn't swim.* (We guess she looked so good, nobody thought to ask.) She could have been fired. As it happened, she wasn't.

. . .

• • •

There was once an audition for a replacement of a chorus boy in a successful Broadway musical. It called for a male dancer who could sing up to a high F, juggle while roller skating, and specified a clothing size, because the producers didn't want to buy new costumes. Over 100 boys showed up.

• • •

Stories of actors who answered "yes" to any inquiry about one or another skill, then ran out and tried to learn it before the first day of shooting, are legendary. If the skill is in that category, don't bother. Maybe this is a pet peeve of ours, but "skills" should be things practiced at a significantly professional level to be taken seriously, and should not be something any other actor could pick up in the few weeks before shooting starts.

EDUCATION & TRAINING

List any academic colleges and professional acting schools you attended, and the degrees you received.

Don't list the year you graduated: It dates you. Ageism does exist. An executive once was extremely impressed with a list of screen credits on a writer, but when he followed it to the end, he found an early 1950s film credit. Figuring the guy had to be at least 70 by now, he put the résumé aside. Doddering or not, a year later the guy wrote an award-winning screenplay, and the executive was looking for work.

List the name of any acting coaches you studied with. Not your high school drama teacher in Wisconsin, but teachers and coaches who are fairly well-known as established and legitimate within the business.

If you can sing—really sing, not just "carry a tune"—say so and list your vocal coach if he or she has an established reputation in the professional community. If your résumé already lists a number of singing roles in musicals, this isn't necessary. They'll get it.

If you dance, list the schools and teachers you studied with. Dancers in New York and Hollywood tend to come from all over, and choreographers who were once dancers probably spent time on the road, and are usually aware of the best teachers from Boston to Vegas. Again, if your résumé already lists a number of musicals in which you danced, this isn't necessary.

Why list your schools and teachers? Same reason you list your directors. "How *is* old professor Litorsky?" is a good question you may hear from the other side of the table. Gives you the opportunity for an intelligent response, to break the ice and chit-chat. But don't get windy. Say something interesting in response and move on.

Skills and education are two categories you can leave off without penalty if you have so many good acting credits the page is getting crowded and hard to format. They can always ask.

PASSPORTS, WORK PERMITS, ETC.

With all the runaway productions—a subject we won't rant about here—being able to work in Canada or Australia can really perk up casting people. By the same token, if you're clearly from Australia, then you'd obviously need a work permit for local productions. Whatever your situation, if it's unusual, say so. And finally...

THE FORMAT

The actual layout of all this information is key, because casting people may give a résumé only a few seconds glance before they make a preliminary judgement. Your info has to be easy to read. They're not going to study it as if it were a French restaurant's menu unless you've made it past a preliminary look-see.

- Put your name at the top, in the center. Don't allow your name to be overshadowed by a looming agency logo. That should go on the right or left side where your contact info belongs.

• • •

We were auditioning several series regulars for a pilot that shot in Canada. About a week before we were scheduled to begin shooting we were told that we had to cast one of our series regular roles with an actor who was Canadian. We had some choices for each role, but had to get creative to figure out which role would be an actor who had Canadian citizenship. An actor came in to audition and casually mentioned that he was Canadian, and so was his roommate, who had been in earlier in the week auditioning for a different role. Although he ultimately didn't get the part, we ended up hiring his roommate for a different role, all because he had casually mentioned their Canadian citizenship. You never know what information could be helpful to you (or your roommate!).

—E.K.

• • •

- Place your union affiliations directly under your name, and your vital statistics on the side opposite your contacts.
- List your credits, followed by your training and education, then your special skills and any additional useful information.
- We don't mean to be dogmatic, or create a one-size-fits-all, universal style. You should be creative. There's really only one big Don't here: Don't be sloppy. Design something neat and clear. In other words, don't be so creative that your résumé is difficult to read. Use a typeface that's fairly standard, not too flowery or fancy. If you can't tell the capital letters from lower case, or the L's from the l's, try something else.
- Many agents insist on using the same design for all their clients. That makes it easy; you don't have to do it yourself, just give them the information and the agent's assistant will type it up. On the other hand, not many of the major agencies actually have developed a good format. We are constantly annoyed by this. And seeing a repetitive style can make our eyes glaze over. See if you can't put your résumé on their letterhead, which is a good compromise. And never allow your agency to type up your credits without double-checking the result over.
- Size matters: 8 1/2" by 11" is maximum; 8" by 10" is minimum.

    The oddity here—we're sure you've spotted it already—is that the standard picture is 8" by 10" and standard résumé paper is 8 1/2" by 11". That they don't match has been the oldest, longest-standing conundrum in the casting business. Some people cut down their résumés to 8" by 10". That can look nice and neat. Some don't. Don't agonize, it makes no difference whatsoever. The only thing we've seen that was unique was a picture enlarged to 8 1/2" by 11," making the face marginally larger than all the others in the pile. This would have been wildly expensive and wasteful years ago, but given digital photography and computers, today's actors have more flexibility.

- The picture and the résumé go back-to-back. Stick them together with glue or double-sided tape. Or, if you're computer savvy, print them out on both sides of good stock paper. We don't recommend stapling them together, because staples come apart easily and catch on other staples and résumés, which makes filing, piling and shuffling a little more difficult.
- No résumé should be more than one page. If you can't fit your enormous body of work onto a single page, choose your best and most recent credits.

Starting on page 42, you'll see a few examples. See which styles you like best. Then use common sense and creativity on yours.

DEMO REELS

A demo reel is a compilation tape of your film and television work, one that any casting director, producer or director can pop into their VCR or DVD. Once rare, it's now almost mandatory. (And, unfortunately, expensive.) It's not unknown for regional theatres to review demo reels of actors, rather than schlep to L.A. or N.Y.C. to hold casting sessions. Sometimes they're even used *in place of* an audition—say you're on location and the casting has to be completed right now.

Television production and casting offices used to have 3/4" tape, but that's going the way of the eight-track. You should have copies on 1/2" VHS tape.

We're sure that DVDs will shortly replace tape, and the latest generation of computers all come with burners and basic editing software. If you've got one of those home-movie-studios-in-a-Mac, great. The advantage—not counting the creative satisfaction of doing it yourself—is that digital images don't become degraded when copies are made, and the result is lighter and more durable.

Most actors will still need to go to a commercial video maker to get a demo reel assembled. Surely it goes without saying that

LAURENCE OLIVIER

5'10"	SAG, British Equity	FINE MGMT
165 lbs		152 Wardour St
		London
		44-2-765-4321

FILM   director:

Clash of the Titans	Zeus	Desmond Davis
The Jazz Singer	Cantor Rabinovitch	Richard Fleischer
Dracula	Van Helsing	John Badham
The Boys from Brazil	Ezra Lieberman	Franklin J. Schaffner
A Bridge Too Far	Dr. Jan Spaander	Richard Attenborough
Marathon Man	Christian Szell	John Schleisinger
Sleuth	Andrew Wyke	Joseph L. Maniewicz
Othello	Othello	John Dexter
Spartacus	Marcus Licinius Crassus	Stanley Kubrick
The Entertainer	Archie Rice	Tony Richardson
Hamlet	Hamlet	Laurence Olivier
Rebecca	de Winter	Alfred Hitchcock
Wuthering Heights	Heathcliff	William Syler

TELEVISION

Peter the Great	King William III	Marvin Chomsky
The Last Days of Pompeii	Gaius	Peter R. Hunt
King Lear	King Lear	Michael Elliot
A Talent for Murder	Dr. Anthony Wainwright	Alvin Rakoff
A Voyage Round My Father	Clifford Mortimer	Alvin Rakoff
Brideshead Revisited	Lord Marchmain Michael	Lindsay Hogg
The Merchant of Venice	Shylock	Jonathan Miller
Long Day's Journey Into Night		
	James Tyrone, Sr.	Michael Plakemore

STAGE

Romeo & Juliet	Romeo & Mercutio	West End
Hamlet	Hamlet	Kronberg Castle,
		Elsinore, Denmark
The Entertainer	Archie Rice	B'way & West End
Private Lives	Victor Prynne	B'way & West End

AWARDS

Oscar Award, best actor, 1948, Hamlet
7 Academy Award nominations, best actor
Knighted 1947, Life Peer 1970
Empire Magazine 1997, "Top 100 movie stars of all time"
2001 Orange film survey of greatest British Actors, ranked 10th

British citizen, has work permit for United States

Though crammed with info, this one is neat and easy to read.

VIVIEN LEIGH

5'3"
110 lbs.

Contact: Myron Selznick
8000 Sunset Blvd.
Beverly Hills, CA
Cashmere 8-3000

FILM ROLES

Ship of Fools .... Mary Treadwell

The Roman Spring of Mrs. Stone Karen Stone

The Deep Blue Sea .... Hester Collyer

A Streetcar Named Desire .... Blanche DuBois

Anna Karenina .... Anna Karenina

Caesar and Cleopatra .... Cleopatra

That Hamilton Woman .... Emma Lady Hamilton

Waterloo Bridge .... Myra Lester

21 Days .... Wanda

Gone with the Wind .... Scarlett O'Hara

Sidewalks of London .... Libby

A Yank at Oxford .... Mrs. Elsa Craddock

Storm in a Teacup .... Victoria Gow

Dark Journey .... Madeleine Goddard

Fire Over England .... Cynthia

Gentlemen's Agreement .... Phil Stanley

Look Up and Laugh .... Marjorie Belfer

Things Are Looking Up .... School Girl

The Village Squire .... Rose Venables

Easy to read, but not enough information.

JOHN CANDY

6'3"   SAG, AFTRA   CAA
250 lbs.

FILMS

Wagons East (1994)—James H. Harlow, Sony Pictures, dir: Peter Markle
Cool Runnings (1993) .... Irving 'Irv' Blitzer, disney, dir: Jon turteltaub
Boris and Natasha (1992)—Kallishak, Showtime, dir: Charles Martin Smith
Once Upon a Crime... (1992)—Augie Morosco, MGM, dir: Eugene Levy
JFK (1991)—Dean Andrews, WB, dir: Oliver Stone
Delirious (1991)—Jack Gable, MGM, dir: Tom Mankiewicz
Only the Lonely (1991)—Danny Fox, dir: Chris Columbus
Uncle Buck (1989)—Buck Russel,l Universal, dir: John Hughes
Who's Harry Crumb? (1989)—Harry Crumb, TriStar, dir: Paul Flaherty
Great Outdoors, The (1988)—Chet, Universal, dir: Howard Deutch
Planes, Trains & Automobiles (1987)—Del Griffith, Paramount, dir: John
Hughes
Spaceballs (1987)—Barfolemew 'Barf,' MGM, dir: Mel Brooks
Little Shop of Horrors (1986)—Wink Wilkinson, WB, dir: Frank Oz
Armed and Dangerous (1986)—Frank Dooley, Columbia, dir: Mark L. Lester
Volunteers (1985)—Tom Tuttle, TriStar, dir: Nicholas Meyer
Summer Rental (1985)—Jack Chester, Paramount, dir: Carl Reiner
Brewster's Millions (1985)—Spike Nolan, Universal, dir: Walter Hill
Splash (1984)—Freddie Bauer, Disney, dir: Ron Howard
Going Berserk (1983)—John Bourgignon, Universal, dir: David Steinberg
National Lampoon's Summer Vacation Vacation (1983)—Lasky, Guard at
Walleyworld, WB, dir: Harold Ramis
Stripes (1981)—Dewey 'Ox' Oxburger, Columbia, dir: Ivan Reitman
Blues Brothers, The (1980)—Burton Mercer, Universal, dir: John Landis
1941 (1979)—Pvt. Foley, Columbia, dir: Steven Spielberg

TELEVISION

The Rocket Boy (1989)
Really Weird Tales (1987)
The Last Polka (1984)
"Tales of the Klondike" (1981) (mini) TV Series
"SCTV Network" (1976-1981) TV Series—Johny LaRue/Billy Sol Hurok/Mayor
Tommy Shanks/William B./Various other Roles
The Courage of Kavik, The Wolf Dog, (1980)

Canadian citizen, work permit for USA

Hard to read.

PAULINE "PEBBLES" TREADWATER

non-union

5'1"   pager: (888) 555-5555
99 lbs

FILMS

Stocks and Bonds—lead
American Booty—guest appearance ("Girl in Handcuffs")
Hannah and her Blisters—supporting role
The Pleasure of Sierra Madre—lead
Citizen Pain—supporting role

TELEVISION

"Ask Pebbles"—host, cable access call-in & variety show

STAGE

Three years at the Blu Ball Saloon—featured dancer

EDUCATION

St. Ignatius School for Girls
Wyoming School of the Arts (BA in theatre)
Marilyn's Mission—completed two year graduate certificate course
in striptease

SPECIAL SKILLS

Horseback riding (bareback), sign language, can touch tip of nose
with tongue.

*Film credits lack info, but this one makes the most out of a
limited career. Don't point out your non-union status—don't
give them any reason not to bring you in for an audition.*

United Talent Agency

Management: One Entertainment
(310) 555-5555

IVANA MILICEVIC

FILM

LOVE ACTUALLY	Supporting	Richard Curtis/ Universal
DOWN WITH LOVE	Supporting	Peyton Reed / Fox 2000
VANILLA SKY	Featured	Cameron Crowe/ Paramount
RUSSIAN JOB	Lead	Robert Capelli/ Independent
HEAD OVER HEELS	Supporting	Mark Waters/ Universal Pictures
LOVE STINKS	Supporting	Jeff Franklin / Independent
ENEMY OF THE STATE	Featured	Tony Scott / Touchstone
OCTOBER 11	Featured	Richard Schenkman / Independent
KISS THE SKY	Supporting	Roger Young / Independent
NO INSURANCE (short film)	Lead	David Baer / Independent
THE BIG BRASS RING (short film)	Lead	George Hickenlooper / Independent
POST MORTEM	Supporting	Albert Pyun / Independent
CRAZY SIX	Supporting	Albert Pyun / Independent

TV

Friends	Guest Star/NBC
The Mind of The Married Man	Series Regular/ HBO
Buffy	Guest Star/ UPN
Off Center	Guest Star/ WB
Men, Women and Dogs	Guest Star/ WB
Nash Bridges	Recurring/ CBS
Secret Agent Man	Guest Star/ WB
The Army Show	Series Regular/ WB
Felicity	Guest Star/ WB
Jersey	Guest Star/ NBC
House Rules	Guest Star/ NBC
Satan's Child	Featured/ ABC
The Nanny	Guest Star/ CBS
Unhappily Ever After	Guest Star/ WB
Seinfeld	Guest Star/ NBC
Babylon	MOW/ UPN
Buzzkill	Featured/ MTV

VIDEO

THIRD EYE BLIND	Dir.: Francis Lawrence

TRAINING

Sandy Marshall - Scene Studies
Larry Moss Studio - Classic Scene Studies
Harvey Lembeck's School of Comedy - Improvisation
The Groundling Theatre - Improvisation
Ivana Chubbuck Studio - Scene Studies

SKILLS

Dialect, Stand-Up Comedy, Tap, Jazz, Modern Dance, Volleyball, Horseback Riding, Skydiving, Skiing, Tae-Kwon Do.

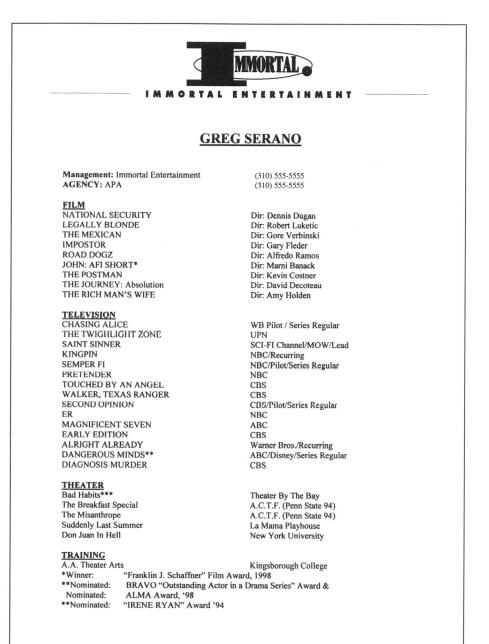

IMMORTAL ENTERTAINMENT

GREG SERANO

Management: Immortal Entertainment   (310) 555-5555
AGENCY: APA   (310) 555-5555

FILM

NATIONAL SECURITY	Dir: Dennis Dugan
LEGALLY BLONDE	Dir: Robert Luketic
THE MEXICAN	Dir: Gore Verbinski
IMPOSTOR	Dir: Gary Fleder
ROAD DOGZ	Dir: Alfredo Ramos
JOHN: AFI SHORT*	Dir: Marni Banack
THE POSTMAN	Dir: Kevin Costner
THE JOURNEY: Absolution	Dir: David Decoteau
THE RICH MAN'S WIFE	Dir: Amy Holden

TELEVISION

CHASING ALICE	WB Pilot / Series Regular
THE TWIGHLIGHT ZONE	UPN
SAINT SINNER	SCI-FI Channel/MOW/Lead
KINGPIN	NBC/Recurring
SEMPER FI	NBC/Pilot/Series Regular
PRETENDER	NBC
TOUCHED BY AN ANGEL	CBS
WALKER, TEXAS RANGER	CBS
SECOND OPINION	CBS/Pilot/Series Regular
ER	NBC
MAGNIFICENT SEVEN	ABC
EARLY EDITION	CBS
ALRIGHT ALREADY	Warner Bros./Recurring
DANGEROUS MINDS**	ABC/Disney/Series Regular
DIAGNOSIS MURDER	CBS

THEATER

Bad Habits***	Theater By The Bay
The Breakfast Special	A.C.T.F. (Penn State 94)
The Misanthrope	A.C.T.F. (Penn State 94)
Suddenly Last Summer	La Mama Playhouse
Don Juan In Hell	New York University

TRAINING

A.A. Theater Arts   Kingsborough College
*Winner: "Franklin J. Schaffner" Film Award, 1998
**Nominated: BRAVO "Outstanding Actor in a Drama Series" Award &
   Nominated: ALMA Award, '98
**Nominated: "IRENE RYAN" Award '94

Because this actor has so much experience, it's assumed that the roles listed under Television are guest star credits unless otherwise specified.

you've saved a copy of everything you ever filmed. If not, ask the director or the producer for clips.

The same rules apply here as when you're looking for a photographer. Do your homework; look at samples. Go to a professional.

Some other guidelines for a compelling demo reel:

- Ten to twelve minutes is about perfect. Fifteen to twenty minutes is probably maximum. Don't go longer than half an hour, and don't count on casting people watching more than the first five minutes.

- A demo reel is not a full film. If you've played the lead in a film or television show, it'll be on your résumé, and if they want to see the whole performance, they'll ask your agent for a copy. Your agent can either refer them to their local Blockbuster, or send over a copy. If it's a fairly obscure independent film that's not on local shelves, make sure your agent has a few DVDs. Sometimes a film hasn't been released on video yet. Often the production company will be able to provide you with a copy before release.

- Put together brief scenes of your best work. Generally in reverse chronological order. No sense in starting with your child actor stuff if you've crossed 30. It goes without saying that the most riveting of your latest work should go first. Remember the five-minute rule. Hollywood people have very short attention spans. (If they wanted to sit still for long periods of time, they would have majored in Russian Literature.)

- Don't reach too far back in your repertoire. If you're pushing 40, that great scene you played when you were 20 is only going to confuse them, or worse, convince them they want a younger actor.

- Include the widest range of material you have. Start off with your headshot, so they can match your tape with your picture and résumé. And always make sure your name is titled at the beginning. Accompanying letters are separated from tapes, never to find their way back again. Which is why you...

- Don't send out a tape that doesn't have your contact info on *both* the box *and* the tape. In production offices, boxes are separated from tapes and lost at a rate of nearly 100 percent.

- Don't get overly creative. A music montage of all your character roles might hold their attention for ten seconds. After that, you're stretching it. They want to see you *act*.
- Don't put anything without dialogue too close to the front, but do include a purely physical scene if it's a good one. Martial arts or acrobatics could attract attention.
- Don't include more than one scene from each project. If you're just starting out, and you only have one good project on film, you'll probably want to select two or three short scenes to compile, so this isn't an absolute no-no. But if your first priority is one riveting scene at the beginning, your second priority should be variety.
- If you've played a good scene in a foreign language you could include it toward the end. Not long, just enough to show your fluency.
- Don't include commercials unless you've got a good bit of real acting in one. Save them for your commercial reel.
- Don't send out anything that is less than broadcast quality in both sound and picture. The video your dad took of your college play is not going to be acceptable.
- Don't ever include a scene in which the other actor or actors outshine you. Unless it's a big star. That you played a scene with Jack Nicholson or Tom Cruise is good, as long as he didn't blow you off the screen. Chances are, however, Nicholson and Cruise got all the close-ups, so be careful not to use something that isn't a good showcase for *you*. If you're an actress, lean towards scenes with actors, if you're an actor, lean towards scenes with actresses.
- If you've got good footage of a stage production, okay, but don't use it unless it's broadcast quality. Even professionally photographed stage productions on PBS can look a bit "hollow," and overly dramatic on television.
- Never give out your original. Almost no one in Hollywood returns scripts or tapes.
- Casting offices will sometimes ask you to come and pick up your tape. Don't hesitate to do so. They're expensive, you don't want to have to make more copies than you have to.

Don't make them call you again. If you don't want to make the trip, tell them it's okay, you have plenty of copies, they can throw it away.

- You've spent good money to get your footage together, don't stint on the editing. Work with a professional to create a good flow of scenes. Place titles over the beginning of each scene, listing the name of the film or television show.

- As with your credits, if you only have a few minutes of film, there's nothing wrong with that. You're a newcomer, and new is often hot in Hollywood.

The picture/résumé and demo reel are important. Be creative, and keep them up to date.

In Short...

- Don't ignore the importance of a quality picture and a clear, informative résumé.

- Don't ever run out of copies of your picture/résumé.

- Don't give out any of the master tapes of your work.

. . . .

- Do keep your résumé up to date.

- Do take copies of your picture and résumé with you to all auditions.

4

Preparing for an Audition

If your agent has secured an audition for you, get a copy of the breakdown, or get the agent's assistant to read your role's description to you over the phone. You'll want to know what the production is looking for, in their own words. There should be sides available—pages from the script for just the scene you're going to read. In that case, get them from your agent as soon as possible. Fax machines make this easy, but if you don't have one, at least have the number of your local Kinko's ready for your agent. Sides are also available on-line in some cases. Showfax.com is an on-line service that carries some breakdown news and sides, and is a good source for student-film casting, which is a decent avenue for young actors hoping to build their demo reels.

There's actually a SAG rule that a script must be available for any audition. It's certainly much easier to get a

• • •

Historical note: In the days of typewriters and carbon copies, "sides" used to be only your lines, with the last few words from the preceding speech as your cue. No sense in typing the whole scene every time. You could even be issued a script of the whole play...with only your character's cues and lines! You might be waiting through a short punch line or a long monologue—you'd never know—while listening for your cue. With the invention of the photocopy machine, "sides" now include all the lines in a scene.

• • •

handle on a role from the full arc of the story than it is from the sides. Your agent or the casting office may provide you with a copy of the script. If not, they will often let you read it, provided you sit in the casting office. Take the opportunity to do so. You'll learn more about the role, and hey, it can't hurt for the casting director to see your face every time she goes out to the bathroom, even if it is buried in a script.

Now, *prepare*. Study the script or sides. Come up with an approach. Read the lines aloud. Take them to your acting teacher or coach if you have the chance. Run them with a fellow actor if you can. If it's a part in an already established series, watch the show for its rhythm and style.

Because auditions are a constant and continuous part of an actor's life, most actors get pretty experienced at them, and sometimes become blasé. This is understandable but dangerous. Don't take any audition for granted, no matter how unlikely you think it is that you'll get the role.

- Know the style of the show you are auditioning for. *Friends* is very different from *Scrubs*. Both are unlike *Sex and the City*. Yet all are considered comedies. An actor should watch at least one episode of every television series. The rhythm and tempo of the show may not be evident in the sides you're asked to read. For example, you may not be able to tell that *Gilmore Girls* is uniformly acted at a rapid pace just from the script.

- Go over your lines. If there's one thing that's more impressive than a good reading, it's a good reading without burying your face in the sides. Many actors will memorize the material if it isn't too lengthy. This could make it possible for you to give a better audition. It frees you to make the eye contact that will enhance your performance.

· · ·

When *Pretty Woman* went into production, the script was far from done and new pages were given the night before. I would call agents at night and have actors arrive at the crack of dawn to the set, audition, and one would be sent to wardrobe. Even while shooting on Rodeo Drive, between takes, I was reading actresses on the sidewalk with Garry Marshall. Be prepared to go anywhere at anytime—you just never know.

—Dori Zuckerman
Casting Director, *What's Cooking?* (feature) and *That's My Bush!* (TV)

· · ·

- If you do memorize your lines, don't let the producers know it. Keep the sides in your hand as you audition. Sometimes when there are no sets, props or costumes, there's not much to do with your hands, and holding the sides or script is useful. Keeps you from looking awkward. At the same time, if you were to give up the sides altogether, you could:

   1) Freeze up (a disaster).

   2) Be expected to give a much more polished performance. It's an audition, not opening night. They expect you to be good, not perfect. They're looking for a quality, and an approach to the role, not a finished performance.

   3) End up "locked in," and not be able to take direction.

- Stay in shape. You never know when you're going to have to show a little skin. Or a lot. If you're in the hunk or bimbo category, make the most of it. But this means all actors, not just the *Baywatch* wannabes. Healthy people radiate energy, and that's the same as charisma for an actor. Join a health club. Find a sport you like. Many actors are lucky; they don't have a 9-to-5 job every day, and can usually make time for classes. Even if you're an overweight character actor, do whatever you can. If your schedule allows, there can be

---

• • •

I like them to be prepared. I like it when they are familiar enough with the material that I see their faces.

—Julie Hughes
Casting Director,
Blood Simple **(feature) and**
The Cosby Show **(TV)**

• • •

• • •

I'm a big one on setting goals, so when I go into an audition, I have a goal and it's not necessarily to get the job. Even if I'm great, if they want someone with a different look, or who matches someone else, or with a different energy, or who is more visible—well, there's nothing I can do about that. But I *can* make a good impression by my energy, preparation, and behavior in the room. If I'm not right for this, but if I've moved someone, it's likely I will be remembered for another time, so I approach the audition as though it were the job. My goal is to do a great job in the room, then I'm happy.

—K Callan
Actress and Author

• • •

nothing more valuable than exercise right before an audition. (Leaving yourself time to shower and catch your breath, of course.) It gets your blood flowing, and sharpens your senses. What better way to walk into an audition?

- Stay in acting shape as well. Acting is supposed to look natural. It's supposed to look easy. It *isn't.* Some of the best acting techniques:

    1) The illusion of ease. Look comfortable, try to be comfortable within your own skin.

    2) The illusion of the first time. (Not so easy when you've heard the same cue every night for a year or two.)

    3) The illusion of power in reserve. (When a great soprano sings a high C, it's great because it *sounds* like she could go even higher.)

    And what acting also isn't, is natural.

The fact is, casting people can tell right away if you're cold, if your elocution is bad, if your breath control is poor, if you're uncomfortable. Our key word: *Confidence.* You'll get it by keeping in practice. Find a good acting teacher and stay with it. Education isn't over because you graduated from the University with a major in Theatre Arts.

Be "up" and ready when you go to an audition. Some people are naturally ebullient. Others require motivational tapes. Do whatever you have to do, but don't fail to prepare your mood as well as your monologue when you have an audition.

> • • •
>
> If I have recommended an actor to a casting director and that actor comes into my audition unprepared, unless there are significant mitigating circumstances (illness or death in the family, say), I will not call that performer back ever again.
>
> —Lloyd Segan
> **Executive Producer,**
> *The Dead Zone*
>
> • • •

- Don't turn down an audition because you think you're wrong for the part. If *they* think you might be right for the role and are willing to hear you try it on for size, go and show them how talented you are. If you give a good audition but are wrong for the role, one of two things will happen. They may re-imagine the role for you. Or they'll remember, and eventually cast you in something else.

If you think they might have mistaken you for someone else ("Are you sure you want *Jake* Nicholson?"), or if you've changed considerably ("I'm nine-months pregnant, will that be all right?") there's time and effort to be saved on all sides by warning them. And you won't be doing yourself a favor if for some reason—say you're going to run the Ironman the day before—you know you're going to do a crappy job. Then you might want to see if you can postpone. If there's been a mistake, you can always laugh it off and say it was good to see you. Generally, go to any audition that will have you. And dazzle them.

Sometimes you just can't get a handle on the part. In that case, it's better to pass on the role. You don't want to give a bad audition because casting directors have long memories. But if you think you can give a good audtion because you feel you can connect with the material, even though you think you're not "right" for the part, then go in and give it your best shot. Make the role into something else. Be bold. Being *wrong* isn't ever really going to go against you. Only being *bad* is—as in boring, artificial, self-conscious or unprepared.

• • •

Dustin Hoffman didn't want to audition for the Bock and Harnick musical *The Apple Tree*, because he couldn't sing. Talked into it, he auditioned. And he couldn't sing. (Alan Alda got the part.) But the director was Mike Nichols, who remembered Hoffman's audition when, not long afterwards, he was searching for a lead for his film *The Graduate*. The rest is history.

• • •

• • •

If an actor truly doesn't feel that he can connect to a character, he should choose *not* to audition. How can a casting director or producer properly evaluate an actor's ability when an actor auditions for a role that he doesn't connect with? It's much better to pass on an audition than to go in and give a *bad* audition. That being said, sometimes it does pay to just take your best shot.

—Kathleen Letterie
**Executive Vice President
of Talent and Casting,
The WB Network**

• • •

YOUR CHECKLIST

When your agent calls with an appointment, be sure to ask enough questions to help you prepare properly. Have copies of a brief questionnaire sitting by your phone. Most of this information is already listed on the breakdown, but if you don't (or can't) get a copy of that from your agent, at least get something like this...

Who am I auditioning for?

Write down the name of the casting director and associate, producer, director, writer, anyone associated with the project who might be there, and what their position is, to the extent that the agent can tell you. Also the studio and/or network producing the project. There's no harm in doing a little research on the principals. The Internet Movie Database (IMDb.com) could give you their credits, as could various *Who's Who* reference books. (No, don't call the director's office and ask, "What has he done?") Screening their work, where possible, could give you a clue to a director's likes and dislikes. Or just casually ask around among your professional friends. "I've got an audition with so-and-so. Any advice?" By checking credits you may find you have someone in common who can give you advice, or at least will be someone to chat about if they want to talk. ("You worked with my friend in Alaska last year...")

What am I auditioning for?

Write down the name of the project, the genre and medium. Is it a sitcom pilot, on-the-air series, feature film, studio or independent, local theatre or on tour, etc. When you prepare a reading, this will be important. You're not going to read Hamlet the same way for a performance at the Opera House as you are for a television special.

What is the style of the project?

Many classic plays will be familiar to you if you're a trained, well-read actor. Continuing series should also be familiar to you. But the entertainment business is full of brand-new scripts. Is this one a comedy or farce, drama or tragedy, period or contemporary, traditional or avant-garde? Any hints can help. You're not going to read a David Mamet character and a Neil Simon character the same way. (And if by some chance the author *is* David Mamet, he's written some books on acting. Do your homework.)

What role am I auditioning for?

Your agent should give you as much information about the role as he has from the casting office or breakdown (again, hopefully, you will get a copy of the breakdown). You may be able to research the character, if it is historical, real, or patterned in some way after an existing role or person.

What level of audition is this?

General meeting, pre-read, callback? Network test? Note what your agent tells you, or what you know. This could affect your reading. If the audition is going to be taped, you might prepare differently, since you'll most likely have less room in which to move around.

Are the sides available now? Is the full script available?

Get the material as soon as possible.

Where and when?

Be precise. Get the correct, detailed address, the date and the time. Misunderstandings happen, and usually there's no harm done, but you don't need to be wasting your energy on stuff like that. Don't wait until the last minute to plan your trip, or your surrounding day's activities.

Here's some very good advice, from people who have seen actors wandering a studio lot in ninety degree heat, looking for an office: Make sure you know where you're going in advance, especially in Los Angeles, where north, south, east and west bear no relationship to reality, and streets are not numbered. Your agent can help with this. So can the casting assistant. If you call that morning, or the day before, the casting assistant will probably be able to give you clear instructions on how to get to the office.

When you're done...

We know we're jumping the gun a little here, but your checklist should also function as a follow-up helper. After the audition, make a few notes on the same page. Cross out anyone who wasn't there, circle anyone you met. Correct any misinformation about the material, and note how well you think you did. File this away. If they call you to come back, you can refer to it, which could help. If there were people there you thought you impressed, put them on your mailing list the next time you send out postcards (more on these later). We know that if you loved bookkeeping, you'd be an accountant and not an actor, but don't allow yourself to become disorganized. This is information that could be important to you in the future.

Okay, you're prepared. Let's go to an audition...

• • •

A brief checklist of thoughts you might tape to the last mirror you're going to look in before you leave for your audition.

1. Do I look as close to the part as I can (without my wardrobe being distracting)?

2. Am I psychologically pumped?

3. Do I have a picture/résumé with me?

4. If I've been given a script or sides, have I...

A) Prepared out loud?

B) Found an interesting approach?

• • •

In Short...

- Don't turn down an audition without a sound reason—every chance to be seen, whether or not you book the job, can help your career.

. . . .

- Do take acting classes to keep your edge.
- Do get the script and sides ahead of time and work with a coach or a friend.
- Do keep track of whom you audition for.

An Actor's Checklist
(make copies and keep this by your phone)

What project am I auditioning for?   ❑ Film   ❑ TV   ❑ Comm   ❑ V.O.

What type of audition is it? ❑ Pre-read ❑ Callback ❑ Straight to Producer(s)

Who am I auditioning for?

Casting Director _____

Producer(s) _____

Director _____

Production company _____

Network _____

What is the style of the project?   ❑ Comedy   ❑ Drama   ❑ Dramedy

What role am I auditioning for?

_____

Character description:

_____

Are the sides available now?   ❑ Yes   ❑ No

Is the full script available?   ❑ Yes   ❑ No

Where and when is the audition?

_____

_____

FEEDBACK_____

_____

5

On Your Way There

You worked hard to land this audition, so make the most of the opportunity by arriving in the proper state of mind. Here are some tips to help you do just that.

- Listen to appropriate music. You're going to get caught in traffic, and you're going to have to find a parking place. The last thing you want to do is arrive tense and angry.
- "Where do I park?" is not an unusual question for Los Angeles, and not an impolite one to ask when you're scheduling an audition. Actually, under SAG guidelines, producers have to supply parking, so if you have to go into a lot, ask if they validate.
- Don't be late. This is especially tricky in Los Angeles, where the studios and production offices are all spread out and the traffic is impossible to gauge. Some actors in Los Angeles have a real laissez faire attitude toward time. In L.A. nine o'clock seems to mean come around nine, take your time, no hurry (this applies to pre-reads, more than producer sessions). With droves of actors going in and out of casting sessions, it's possible that casting people won't even know that you're late (but the assistant will). But if you should keep them waiting at all, they're going to wonder about your professionalism. If you find yourself sitting

behind a steaming car half an hour away from somewhere you should be in five minutes, cell phones make it easy. Call and apologize. The assistant can sometimes re-shuffle appointments and her boss won't even know.

- If you are noticeably, clearly, late, apologize. Don't make a big thing of it. Use a decent excuse—"Spielberg decided he wanted to hear me read three additional scenes"—or nothing at all. But at least say, "I'm sorry to keep you waiting."

- Don't drink alcohol, too much coffee, smoke, do drugs, or eat a heavy meal before an audition. If the role calls for a drunk scene, act. You want to be in complete control, and at your best. Drugs—even perscription drugs like Valium—can hurt your performance. They only make you *think* you're witty and smart. More than one musician has recorded hours of great music while stoned, only to find out the next day that they'd laid down nothing but garbage. Mind altering substances that make you see everything in slow motion, make us see you in slow motion.

> • • •
>
> If an actor is late and I have to wait for him/her, that actor will now have to work even harder to get—and keep—my attention. Don't be late.
>
> —Paul Stupin
> **Executive Producer,**
> *Dawson's Creek*
>
> • • •

YOU'RE ALMOST IN THE DOOR...

Every actor has to spend time in the waiting room. There are a few simple waiting-room rules here, mostly in the category of good manners (which aren't popular these days, but if you want the job...).

- Don't lose your patience. Especially if they are running behind. Find a distraction, a way to use your energy.

> • • •
>
> A young actor waiting to read for producers in my office made an off-hand remark to another actor that the script was awful. He didn't realize that the writer-director was standing within earshot. When he walked into the reading room and discovered his *faux pas*, it was too late.
>
> —Paul G. Bens, Jr.
> **Casting Director,**
> *Murder in Small Town X,*
> *Malcolm and Eddie*
>
> • • •

• • •

Years ago, during a particularly frustrating pilot season, I was exhausted and disappointed by the kind of material I was considered "right" for. I'd been on two auditions that day, and—as I changed my clothes, yet again, in a busy parking lot—I wished I'd gone to college. What was I thinking? "Sometimes you're the windshield and sometimes you're the bug," I reasoned as I signed in at the front desk and grabbed a seat, determined to give it my all.

No sooner had my butt hit the chair than a cranky casting assistant appeared announcing that there was new material for us to read. I tried not to look annoyed as I studied the humorless pages. Where did these people get off putting actors on the spot like this? I'd worked my tail off on this audition and now all the preparation was for nothing! Arggggggggg! Oh well...it's sink or swim. Minutes later it was my turn to read, and as I finished the first scene, pleased I'd managed to remember all my lines, a gruff looking man in the back of the room burst my bubble, barking: "No! No! No! Make it FUNNY...we want FUNNY...!"

"I'm an actress, not a magician," I thought...and suddenly realized from the looks on their faces that I'd said it out loud! "Ah...ha..ha...I mean, just ahh...kidding.... See, I can be funny." No one was laughing. The damage done, I was thanked for my time and excused. I made it to my car and burst into tears. Flash forward to two pilot seasons later. I'm told that the writer-producer of a particular project doesn't want to see me because he thinks I have "attitude." You guessed it—same guy.

Moral of story: Writers are sensitive creatures.

Memo to self: Nothing nice to say, say nothing at all.

—Traci Lords, Actress

• • •

(Though be careful of getting overly hyped up in the waiting room.) Bring a Walkman, study your sides, read a book.
- Don't stray too far from the waiting room. The casting director doesn't want to have to hunt you down.
- Don't dis the script, any of the people involved, or any fellow actors, present or not. Walls have ears.
- Don't get involved in the psych-out game with other actors up for the part. ("You haven't worked in a while, have you?" "I wonder why they see both of us in this role?") It's a waste

of your energy. If someone else is playing it, leave the room for a moment and sit somewhere else when you get back.

- Don't talk too loud. Other actors may be studying their lines or going over their approach. (The ones with their eyes closed are either doing that, or sleeping. Either way, they'd like some quiet.) The assistant may be working the phones. Anyway, why aren't *you* concentrating?
- Don't make a mess. There are trash cans for your Starbucks and Coffee Bean cups. The assistant wants to go home on time, too.
- Don't hesitate to ask for water if you need it. It's the least they can do.
- Don't forget to bring the script or sides they gave you. They don't want to dig out another set, and you don't want any confusion over what you prepared. (Sometimes there has been a mistake, and you find yourself looking at unfamiliar pages. Don't hesitate to say you've never seen this scene before, and ask for a few minutes alone to go over it.) Double-check the sides they gave you against the ones in the waiting room. Dialogue lines may have been added or deleted.

• • •

Do not listen to other actors' auditions through the door. It will make you rethink your choice and destroy your own reading.

Go with your instincts (your original plan) and do your best. Don't psyche yourself out.

—Scott Baio, Actor

• • •

• • •

Never pooh-pooh theatre training and experience. We were casting a Movie of the Week with a very prominent theatre director from England. When an actor came in, he would immediately turn over the résumé and talk about the theatre experience. This director didn't care if you had two Oscars to your name. For him, it was all about being on the stage. One actor walked in, and the director looked at his résumé and said, "Oh my, you don't have any theatre on your résumé." The actor responded with, "And thank God I haven't had too!" Needless to say, he didn't get the job.

—Dori Zuckerman
Casting Director,
What's Cooking? **(feature) and**
That's My Bush! **(TV)**

• • •

- Don't forget to bring a copy of your picture/résumé. Your agent probably sent them over, but you never know. You need only offer them if they are requested.
- You can ask to use the telephone if you need to—there's usually an extension in the office—but it's really more polite to use your own cell phone these days (now that everyone is practically expected to have one). And use it outside. (See, "Don't talk too loud.") If you have to use theirs, make it brief and businesslike. Don't gossip with your mother about where you are and who's here within earshot of the assistant.
- Observe common cell-phone etiquette. Turn off your personal pager or cell phone before you go in to audition. You run the risk of throwing everyone off, especially yourself.
- Don't get caught snooping the office for other projects/roles you want to be seen for. Of course, information is power in show biz, so anything you pick up might be useful. The key is not to get caught.
- Don't make enemies. Again, be nice to the assistants. They can do a lot for you. Some of them have the ear and respect of the casting director. Some have been known to slip an actor a script that wasn't supposed to be available yet. All of them handle the calendar, which can be a big help or a big hurdle, depending on your day. All of them want to be promoted, and when they are, will they remember you? Same with your fellow actors; they can tip you off to all sorts of useful info.

In you go...

In Short...

- Don't be late.

. . . .

- Do be polite.

6

The Cattle Call

Before we get to actually reading for a part, we might as well tell you about the cattle call, theatrical slang you'll understand immediately the first time you attend one.

Although going through existing lists and sifting through agency submissions is one way to start the search for the right actor, another way is the open call. This is quite common in the theatre, where Actors' Equity Association has won in negotiations the demand that certain projects, depending on the contract, spend a certain amount of time seeing anyone who wants to be seen. As onerous, even useless, as this must have seemed to the producers when they gave this concession to the union, it has turned out to be a terrific opportunity for the girl who has just arrived from Nebraska having played the lead in her class musical to at least be seen without even an agent. And a useful method for producers to scout new talent.

If you've seen early episodes of *American Idol*, you have an idea of what a cattle call is like. Hundreds of hopefuls line up for a private, one minute appearance in front of someone who has the power to send you on to the next round.

And by the way, if you're ever going to audition for anything, it isn't a bad idea to watch *American Idol*. You can learn a lot about the audition process by observation. There are lots of ways to make a mistake, and *American Idol* seems to get strong ratings by show-ing you as many as possible. The good news is that no one in the business is as rude as Simon (as least not to your face). It's obvi-ous that the *Idol* judges are *acting for the cameras;* the people for whom you will auditon in real life are not acting. You probably won't ever have to put up with being told you are quite possibly the most dreadful singer in the world. "Thank you," is about the worst thing you'll hear. Still, by the end of the process, a handful of terrific young singers have been skimmed off the top. Which is why the cattle call isn't an exercise in futility for either side, how-ever slow and painful it might be for both.

How to behave at a cattle call? Not much to advise you on here, just a few basics:

- Don't lose your patience, it's going to be a long day. Many actors take a book along with them. This can make the time go faster, keep your mind off the looming disaster and help calm your nerves.
- Don't go unprepared. As many as half of the hopefuls may get to read, or sing or dance before the day is through. So be as "up" as possible and be ready when your moment to shine arrives.
- Don't ignore instructions. If they say go in, give your name and sing one chorus, don't rush in blurting out that you loved the director's last show and you're a really good singer but you left your music at your aunt's birthday party last night and you have a cold but if you could just have a moment with the piano player you'll figure out a mutually satisfactory key in which to sing an obscure Noël Coward song even though you know this is a rock show and.... Follow instructions. Be patient, stay calm, and whatever you do, don't schedule another appointment for later in the day. You won't make it.

In Short...

- Don't lose your patience.
- Don't go unprepared.
- Don't ignore instructions.

7

The "General" Audition

For the general audition, be prepared to chat—just a little—about something interesting. It's simply an informal interview. They might ask how you are, or what your last job was, but they don't really want to know. They just want to see and hear you relaxed, as yourself. If you have practiced a little story with a punch line, make sure it sounds spontaneous. Don't force it into the conversation. They'll know it's a routine of yours, and it will have the opposite effect.

Be yourself. Be real. George Burns once said the secret to success in Hollywood is "sincerity—if you can fake that, you've got it made." A casting director just wants to get a look at you in person. Maybe she's seen your work and wants to know who's behind it. Maybe your agent has insisted she meet you. Maybe you're on someone else's list and the casting director hasn't heard of you. Name actors are often treated this way, on the assumption that their work is already well known. (Truth be told, most actors would rather read than chit chat.) This can happen often at commercial auditions as well.

Be yourself? Sounds like ideology from a '60s guru. Who are we? Do we ever really know? We're different people to our parents than we are to our friends, to our employers than we are to our employees, to our teachers than we are to our fellow students.

Possibly the process of growing up and maturing is simply focusing on becoming the "ourself" with which we're most comfortable. If you're an actor or an artist of any kind you may very well be one of those people whom Merle Miller, in his outstanding book on the craziness of the television business, *Only You, Dick Daring*, described as "born to run away from home." Which means that after spending years finding your true self, you go home for the holidays and revert to becoming exactly the person you left home to get away from being.

But enough with the psychology. Perhaps you're an actor because you're happier being someone else. Many great actors are blank slates in real life, that's what makes them so versatile. Most stars, however, who have forged a successful character in television or film and continue to mine gold with it, are the opposite. They brought their character with them to Hollywood, and it is the underlying sub-text of every role they play. So perhaps we should alter "be yourself" to something more useful. How about, "relax." Don't be nervous. Be genuine.

Oh, sure, easy for us to say. You need this role. You want this role. You would die for this role.

Let us tell you the single most important piece of advice you'll ever get. If you can do this one thing, you have a real chance at that role:

Show confidence.

Don't be arrogant. Don't be obnoxious. Don't be purposefully eccentric. Don't be full of yourself. Nobody wants to work with a self-centered egomaniac—until you're a star and they have to work with you.

The actor who appears to be nervous, who looks as if he lacks self-confidence, or, worse, experience, is almost never going to garner much interest.

You see, it's the inexperience that gives the people with your fate in their hands the willies.

Half a century ago Dale Carnegie popularized the simple concept of a self-fulfilling prophecy in his book, *How to Win Friends and Influence People*. To do well, you must believe you're going to do well. Social scientists have since proven this categorically.

Optimistic people do better than pessimistic people. If you don't believe you can play this character, how will you make others believe it?

Sure, we all know good actors who disparage their own talent, great writers who think everything they've written is garbage. They're acting. You can bet that underneath that beguiling modesty and the poor-me pose, is a self-confident artist who radiates success when in an audition.

Some actors are relieved when they get eliminated. It's a strange psychological phenomenon, but we've seen it many times. They've done their duty for the day, applied for the job and, because they didn't get called back, don't have any further responsibilities. Needless to say, that's a loser's game.

Once in a while, a relatively new young actor may come along who is shaking with fear, and it shows all over, and yet there is something about him

> • • •
>
> When Garry Marshall was casting the role of The Fonz for *Happy Days*, they were looking for a 6' tall, blond, attractive Italian guy. Henry Winkler, a short, Jewish, dark haired actor walked in and blew them all away. He made great choices with the character and won the role.
>
> • • •

or her that is perfect for the role. A good casting director or director may spot some talent, or just some appropriateness for the role, and work with them a bit. If they blossom as they gain confidence, they might end up with the role. Casting people are used to seeing a bundle of nerves in front of them, and the best know how to put you at ease. But first impressions are important. Ninety-nine times out of one hundred, anyone who doesn't appear to be an *experienced professional* is going to get tossed without much ado. And when an actor comes along who seems to command the stage or room (with or without experience), our eyes and ears perk up at once. Because the difference is as clear as a bell.

We'll admit this is not the easiest thing to do. Everyone is nervous. There's a way to put your nerves aside. We're sure that's what great athletes do. You can't play the game of a lifetime without being nervous, but you can't sink a last minute three-pointer if you're *thinking* that it's the game of a lifetime. Focus on the immediate job at hand. One age-old piece of advice for people on stage is to imagine that everyone in the audience is in their underwear.

Probably the theory is that they won't seem so intimidating then. We won't recommend anything so specific—sexual harassment law suits being all the rage these days—but you get the idea. It won't hurt to remember that the people behind the desk are living the same volatile, edge-of-disaster life that you are.

If the production doesn't use the time-honored cattle call for a first round of auditions, the casting director will probably call in a number of actors for a reading. Well, not quite a reading. It's generally called...

In Short...

• Don't appear nervous.

• Don't be arrogant.

. . . .

• Do exude confidence.

8

The Pre-Read

For films, television, and once in a while the stage, you'll be asked to read for the casting director before you get to read for anyone else connected with the production. It's the casting director's job to screen the talent pool for the best actors for each role. This may actually be your most important audition. After all, the producer or director is only casting one project. The successful casting director may have several projects at any given time. Moreover, if you deliver a good audition, you will be remembered for next time.

We'll say it again: This could be your most important level of audition. If you can't get past the casting directors in town, you're not going anywhere fast. But if a casting director becomes enamored with your talent, you're going to get a lot of important auditions. The casting director *loves* to discover new talent. The casting director hopes that you will turn out to be terrific. Think about it. Her job is to deliver a great actor in every role. She can't wait for the right person to come in and read well. Don't think of any audition, but especially not the pre-read, as an obstacle. Think of it as an opportunity.

A few guidelines for the pre-read:

- Feel free to ask specific (brief) questions about the character.

- Don't ask the casting director to tell you about the whole project—read the script.
- Don't ask the casting director if you're getting a callback.
- Tell the casting director if you are committed in the near future, or are going out of town.
- Though it doesn't often happen, sometimes the casting director will tell you then and there if you are being called back. Ask her if you should wear the same outfit, and be clear on any direction she may have given you so you can prepare the same performance for the producer.

9

A Short "Commercial" Break

A unique (and very lucrative) part of the business is commercials. Commercial actors are brought in by the casting director and given the "script," which could be anything from a full scene to reactions to a product. "Improvisation" is actually against SAG rules, because advertising agencies used to ask talented actors and comedians to improvise, then used their ideas to script the commercial, while hiring someone else. Nevertheless, very often actors are encouraged to "embellish" the script, that is, told they have the freedom to add lines or physical bits as they choose. Improv classes should be part of your training. Commercial actors can get very good at this, and many can come in and quickly nail a script, identifying the comic beats and giving a superb reading. The casting director then chooses a handful of the applicants for a callback, which will also be attended by the commercial director, probably advertising agency representatives, and sometimes the client. There is in some circles an assumption that commercial actors are not "real" actors, but this is an arrogant and unfair premise. The quality of work in commercials, in all categories from the creative to the technical, often overshadows that of the shows they support (as anyone who has watched the Super Bowl can attest). If you are interested in commercials, you'll need an agent who specializes in them, a commercial composite picture, and eventually, a commercial reel. But our primary focus here is long-form acting, so we'll now return to our regularly scheduled program.

10

Wardrobe and Grooming

WARDROBE

When it comes to wardrobe, some actors go all out, to the point of renting a civil war uniform for a costume-drama audition. Others feel they should rely on their acting, and wear an "actor's" outfit. (These days, a seemingly unendless parade of grubby T-shirts with baggy jeans for men and tiny T-shirts with low-cut jeans for women.)

Both approaches miss the point. Go ahead, dress the part. But...

- Don't let your clothes upstage you. Your appearance should not be more memorable than your audition. Heavy cleavage and ultra-tight clothes are distracting.
- Don't wear wild colors or wacky patterns. Don't distract from your face.

• • •

I once had an actor come in for a pre-read wearing a nice silk suit, an excellent choice because the character was hip and upscale. His reading was good and he was given a callback. When he came in to read for the producers, he was wearing a ripped tank top, ripped bike shorts and a hat. He looked as if he had just come from the gym. When he left, my producers turned to me and said, "Why would an actor wear that for this kind of role?" He gave everyone the impression that he simply didn't care about the audition.

—E.K.

• • •

• • •

When I auditioned for the roll of Martha Kent on *Lois and Clark: The New Adventures of Superman*, I had a dilemma. I like to dress like the character for auditions because it feeds me as an actor. When I read the script, I thought of all the things we think about Martha Kent and decided I should wear a little printed shirt with an easy skirt and my hair back in a bun. But there was a scene in the script where Martha welds. And I just kept thinking how I really felt like Martha; I do all those things: build, saw, design. I caught sight of a picture of myself with my grandchildren dressed as I am at home when I'm working in the garage. I had on sweats, a red turtleneck T-shirt and my hair all scraggly. That's how I wanted to go in, but I was really worried about doing it because it was such a departure from what we traditionally think about Martha. I actually dressed myself in both outfits to decide. When I put on the sweats, I knew that was right. When I arrived at the audition, every other actress in the room had her hair in a bun with a little blouse and skirt. It was scary to go so far out on a limb, but also invigorating (even if I hadn't scored the part, which I did!). I have had other auditions that didn't turn out that well, but I always had a good time even when I left and people were scratching their heads about my choices. At least I made a choice. That's the hardest part.

—K Callan
Actress and Author

• • •

- Wear something to help you get into character, but don't try too hard. It smacks of amateurism to show up in scrubs for a doctor role. If you're up for the part of a Swiss Bell Ringer, wearing lederhosen may be going a little too far. (Maybe not. Comedy comes in many guises.) But there's no sense in wearing a three-piece suit if you're up for a sun-addled surfer. The key here is to wear something that suggests the role, but doesn't distract from your performance. (Angelenos are lucky here, as they can arrive by private car. It's tough for actors to take the subway dressed like the Easter Bunny, though we've seen it.)
- Don't wear clothing that shows sweat stains. You might sweat at an audition, and unless you're up for the role of a

basketball player and the scene is the game, it's probably going to be distracting. (A little deodorant won't hurt nervous actors either.)

GROOMING

Hair and makeup are in the costume category. That is, go for the role, but stay within reasonable limits. Your normal hair style should be flattering and, if possible, relatively flexible. This is easier for women than men, because women with long hair can tuck it up, ponytail it, let it all hang out. Hair pieces can be useful. Men have more difficulty, though you can always try to brush it into something approximating what you think the character would do. Don't do anything that attracts attention to itself, only as much as you can to support the time, place and character behind the role. We've seen some extraordinarily good wigs on women, wigs which we didn't know were wigs until they got the role. On men, hairpieces, toupees and wigs usually look just as fake as they are. It seems to be awfully hard to get a truly natural look. If you're bald and wear a wig, make sure it's a really, really good one. And have pictures of yourself both with and without. There are plenty of bald characters, and you should be prepared to play both at the drop of, well, a wig. Moustaches are, like hair, a personal choice. If you like the way you look with a beard or moustache, who are we to tell you to shave? The production may ask. Be willing, or be prepared to tell them you won't. Be sure to have pictures of your face with and without.

• • •

An actor who had worn a beard for his regular role throughout seven years of a successful series later went to an audition clean-shaven, and wasn't recognized. This worked to his advantage, as the producers didn't want a recognizable personality from television for this particular film role. In general, however, he was caught in a catch-22 situation. If he wore the beard in his post-series career, he took advantage of his celebrity to gain work, but was typecast. If he was clean-shaven he was virtually unrecognizable, and presented a much wider range of type, but had to audition as if starting his career from scratch.

• • •

Where makeup is concerned, men should not wear any to an audition. Women should use no more than their regular street makeup—a category in which we think "less is more" is appropriate—unless you are specifically going for a unique look, a character you believe would layer it on.

If you need glasses to see the script, wear them. If you also have contacts, good, that will make you more versatile. Don't get caught squinting at pages. It will ruin your rhythm, and it will tell them you're an actor who can't even remember to bring his reading glasses. Some actors have prop glasses that make them look more intelligent or studious, but have only plain glass in them. This could be useful for certain roles.

Don't wear your hair over your face, or dark glasses, or low hats that hide half your face, or a hooded sweatshirt with the hood covering all but your nose. If they can't see your expression, they aren't going to see your talent.

Don't wear any jewelry that is going to sound like a musical accompaniment when you move. Don't put on a lot of perfume or cologne—it smells up the room and is distracting (also, you won't make a good impression if you trigger an allergy attack).

· · ·

Please don't "dress the part." Just bring yourself to the audition. If the part calls for a "Goth Teenager," please don't show up looking like a mini Marilyn Manson. Likewise, if the part calls for anyone in any type of uniform, don't. Let the focus be on you, not your clothes. Dress simply and tastefully. In fact, the simpler the better. But whatever you choose to wear, make sure you're comfortable.

—Constance Burge,
**Creator of *Charmed*;
Writer for *Ed, Boston Public,
Ally McBeal***

· · ·

Well, if you're not prepped now, you'll never be. Let's get to...

In Short...

• Don't walk into an audition overly made up or overly scented.

. . . .

• Do wear clothes you are comfortable in.

11

The Big Read

Okay, you're in the door!

Rule Number One: You are auditioning from the moment you walk in the door, until the moment you walk out the door.

Rule Number Two: This is your turn, your time. Use it to your advantage.

- Don't unpack. Travel light. If you're wearing coats, scarves, gloves and other layers you will not want to read in, take them off in the waiting room. Leave your coffee and danish outside. Enter the room with *only* your sides and *one* bag that can hold all your valuables and personal effects. Don't unpack.

- Don't take over the room. Casting people generally think you're wasting their time if you spend a lot of it rearranging the furniture. A reading is just that, *a reading*. It's not a performance. In fact, casting people can get suspicious if you give

> • • •
>
> We were auditioning actresses with a scene that had the character cleaning up after a party. This actress came in and started to stack up my chairs in my office. It became less about her audition (or acting ability) and more about wondering where she was going to stack the next chair.
>
> —Paul Stupin
> **Executive Producer,**
> *Dawson's Creek*
>
> • • •

too finely honed a performance. They think you've peaked, and you're not going any further with the role.

- If the director asks you for your credits, give him your résumé. He may not have it in front of him.
- You don't have to fawn. Fawning is clearly a sign of nervousness, and doesn't impress people. Of course you loved the director's last film. Everybody did. Don't be obvious about it.

   On the other hand, don't forget that nobody is immune to flattery. Certainly not in Hollywood. If you saw the director's _first_ film, some obscure festival thing in black and white made for $2,000 that only three people actually saw, and you have something interesting to say about it and you get the chance, go for it. Shows you're hip to films, and to the director. We'll repeat this because it requires a delicate balance: Nobody is immune to flattery, but excess—even in Hollywood—can be irksome.

- Don't stall. Another tricky one. The tempo of casting sessions changes hourly, depending on the backup, the type of session, the personalities involved, etc. You won't know that, and it's hard to judge. You don't want to delay them, but you don't want to rush yourself either. The best advice is simply to answer their preliminary questions with reasonable—not voluble—sentences, and take your cues from them.

- Don't be difficult to work with. This is a volatile topic. Any number of actors over the years have had that reputation. Some have survived it, some have not. Some have deserved it, some have not. Most actors who are hard to work with are in denial, thinking that they're simply perfectionists with strong opinions. The more successful the actor, the more the creators and producers are willing to put up with him or her. So the theory is to get to a certain level of the

• • •

I hate when an actor comes in to audition and begins by lowering his head and "preparing." The preparation should happen _before_ that actor walks through the door. Also, when actors end the audition by saying, "scene," it screams drama school and amateur, not professional actor.

—Paul Stupin
Executive Producer, _Dawson's Creek_

• • •

profession before becoming belligerent over your wardrobe. It may even be true that a male actor can get away with more than an actress, under the classic complaint about sexism: that strong-minded men are defined as leaders, while strong-minded women are labeled bitches. An audition is a mini version of a good collaboration between an actor and a director, and even if the director is not there, everyone knows this. In terms of behavior, they assume that what they see in the room is what they'll see on the set.

- Don't arrive in character. This is a pretty tricky issue, because more than one very successful method actor has taken to staying in character throughout a shoot. And it's not that uncommon for an actor who has prepared his audition to arrive auditioning. The trouble with this technique is that the casting directors don't know it's not you. Most people who are casting want to know who *you* are first. It's *you* they'll have to work with, and everyone hopes for a pleasant working environment. If they already know and appreciate you, you have a little more leeway. But if you played an irascible jerk in a recent film, and even if they're calling you in for a similar role, to show up acting like a jerk from the moment you walk in the door is dangerous. One, nobody wants to work with a creep, and two, you're going to get typecast. Wouldn't it be

• • •

If you have a bad temper (or are starting to lose your patience) and have been waiting a long time at an audition and feel that you are too angry or frustrated to do your best, walk away. Ask if you can reschedule the audition for another day. It's better to do that than to give a bad audition and possibly blow your cool during the reading.

—Scott Baio, Actor

• • •

• • •

According to Hollywood legend, when Dustin Hoffman and Laurence Olivier were working together on *Marathon Man*, Hoffman had a scene where he was supposed to be exhausted. He didn't sleep for two nights previous. When he arrived ready to play the scene, he was haggard and drawn. Olivier said to him, "Why don't you try acting, dear boy."

• • •

• • •

I was casting a television series and we were looking for the "bad guy" guest star of the week. The director of the episode asked me to bring in a friend of his to audition for this role. I wasn't familiar with this actor but, of course, brought him in for the producer's session. Since the character was not only a "bad guy" but also insane, and this actor usually got hired to play "normal, good guy" parts, he thought it would be clever to arrive in character. He was rude and acting "crazy." The problem was that nobody knew he was in character. He came off as rude and odd and someone to be leery of. He not only didn't get that part, but we weren't sure if the actor had the ability to really separate the character from himself. Would he act that way on the set if we hired him? Who wants to take a risk like that?

—E.K.

• • •

better if, after playing the meanest son of a bitch in the valley in your last gig, you showed up as a sweet guy?

• In fact, don't look to play a "character" in the first place. Be yourself, and *as yourself*, play the part. Actors are far more effective—both in auditions and in roles—when they *do* things, rather than try to *be* things. (More on this in Chapter 13.)

• If you have the flu, good for you for showing up anyway. But don't shake anyone's hand. In fact, sick or healthy, shake hands only when they're offered. If more than three people are waiting, try to avoid shaking hands at all costs. If you don't get around to some of them, they'll feel slighted. If you get around to all of them, you've wasted ten minutes of your fifteen minutes of fame.

• • •

I'm not a small-talk kind of producer. A simple hello will do. Some minimal discussion is appropriate if the actor has questions about the role or sides, but they are there to audition, not to be my friend.

—Lloyd Segan
Executive Producer,
The Dead Zone

• • •

• Ask questions. Most producers and casting directors welcome this. Anything you're unsure of, particularly about the scene or your character. ("Is this guy really stark naked all the time?" "You think he smokes?") When they answer your question, make sure you're able to use that in your audition.

If you can't, you probably shouldn't have asked; if you can, make sure it is subtle yet visible in your reading. You may not have any questions, particularly if you've done your homework, and that's okay. ("I think I understand this character. Why don't I read it through once, and then you tell me if you'd like something else?")

But don't ask frivolous questions. Don't ask them to explain the whole story, or tell you all about your character. They don't have the time, and you should have already gotten that information.

- Don't sit down, unless there's a convenient chair and they want to chat, unless it's part of the scene. But be careful when you do. You want to use all your physical energy playing the scene. Don't get stuck in a chair and then, not knowing when to rise, end up playing your big speech stuck to a chair when you had planned something more physical.

- Don't get too physical. Go as far as you like, actually, as long as you don't: 1) break anything, 2) touch anyone, or 3) hurt anybody, especially the person you're reading with. Once an actor in the height of his passion leapt up on the table the casting people were sitting behind and played out the scene. No harm done, and it was actually a very arresting reading. But other actors have virtually bruised the poor volunteer reading with them. If you lose control in the audition, the producers will be concerned about you losing

That's My Bush callbacks with the producers were on the Sony lot, on camera, and I had to read with them. Because the show was sometimes so outrageous, it helped the actors to have me sit in the scene as opposed to reading off camera. One audition required the actors to speak the whole scene in German, so I really didn't know what they were saying. One actor went way off book and found it "appropriate" to lean around me, spit his lines at me, and kiss me. I wanted to kill him. Never touch the reader, and if you have to do a scene up close with someone, have the courtesy to carry Altoids. I will never have that actor in again.

—Dori Zuckerman
Casting Director,
What's Cooking? **(feature) and**
That's My Bush! **(TV)**

control on the set. And, if an actress or casting director ends up with a torn blouse, you could end up with a lawsuit on your hands.

- Often the person reading with you is the casting director, associate or stage manager, and they're sitting behind the desk, or in some other way indicating that they're *just reading*. This can be common, actually, because some directors feel they don't want to see two actors at once. If they've hired an actor to read all day, or the stage manager is doing it, even though the person is standing right there next to you, he or she may have been told not to act, but to just read the lines as simply as possible, to give you your cues. You can't always tell if the assistant is *not* acting, or just plain lousy. Either way, always give it your best.

- Generally, don't smoke, drink, eat, or chew gum unless the script demands it. It's too distracting for the casting people. Smoking is the most common, but it's impolite—and illegal in most public buildings. If you absolutely must play the character with a cigarette, okay, but don't light up. A bottle of beer? Okay, if the script calls for it, but make it root beer and don't spill on their carpet—even better, use an empty bottle.

- Don't bring props, unless you really want to play the scene with one. In that case, it must be *unobtrusive*. It must not become a scene about a prop.

If a scene calls for a prop, you can usually mime it. This is tough to do, however, because actors without real pantomime training tend to look foolish pretending they're, say, dialing a phone. And actors with real pantomime training do it so well that it's their pantomime and not their acting that will get kudos. When we need a Marcel Marceau, we'll call you. An example of a useful prop might be a telephone. If, for example, you need (in the scene) to make a call, you

> • • •
>
> It's always a bad idea to bring the producer "into" the scene. Especially if it's an intimate scene. If an actor looks at me during the audition (instead of the person they are reading with), it makes me feel uncomfortable and I can't focus on the actor's performance.
>
> —Paul Stupin
> **Executive Producer,**
> *Dawson's Creek*
>
> • • •

could whip out your cell phone (make sure it's off), play the scene, then put it back. It would seem natural and probably not distracting. Your best approach is to avoid the use of props wherever you can, real or imaginary. If you must use one, use it minimally.

- On stage, an actor has to be careful with food. A mouthful of potatoes can cripple a punch line. On camera, reality is preferable. However, you shouldn't be asked to eat anything at an audition. (For commercials, you may have to eat something. Make sure you know what it is.)

- Don't direct any other actors in the scene, no matter how much you think you can help them. And don't let them direct you. (And especially watch out for lines like, "Are you really going to play it that way?" That's not directing, that's the psych game. (See waiting-room rules, in Chapter 5.)

- Don't attempt an accent unless you absolutely must. No matter how good you think you are, the performance always becomes *about* the accent, rather than the character.

- Don't feel obligated to always follow the acting instructions in the script if you feel like they are wrong or uncomfortable for you. If the script calls for you to do something, like faint, or shoot someone, you'll have to do it, of course. But when you come across instructions to an actor, as in parenthetical coaching such as (happily) and (with disdain), you can try them, but ultimately go your own way. Just make sure "your own way" doesn't change the intent of the character or of the scene. A good script doesn't tell an actor how to act. A good script provides dialogue and actions that express character so clearly it doesn't need explanation.

- Many actors start too slowly. This is generally because they have left out of their preparation the question of what the character was doing prior to the scene. As a good actor, you must imagine where the character has come from physically and psychologically before your first scene. Don't fail to play this as part of your first moments.

Let's get to the meat of the audition, already...

- Don't wait for anyone to tell you how to play the part. Come up with your own take on the character. Sometimes the breakdown or casting director will have some new information for you, sometimes you'll be given that information just before you read. It's not often the case in Hollywood, however, that you get really good, really specific information. That's okay, because the less specific the role appears, *the more you're able to invent.* Come up with something interesting. Anything is better than nothing. Bring something to the role that makes you stand out, even if it is just your take on a word or a line. Let them know that you're an imaginative, enthusiastic, inventive actor.

This is *very* useful in sitcom pilots. Some writer-producers of sitcoms are open to tailoring a role to a specific actor if he or she brings something to the role that they hadn't thought of. The development process sometimes continues well into the first season and most sitcoms take an entire first season to settle on well-defined formats and characters. Take a look back at the pilot of almost any very successful show. You'll see characters still feeling their way. Good writing inspires actors, but actors—especially in a developing series—inspire good writers, too.

Commercials also leave you a lot of room. Take it. Commercial directors generally encourage an actor's contribution. There's more time to shoot, and they love to go into the editing room with a lot of choices.

• • •

Actors shouldn't be afraid to make choices, even if it's a "wrong" choice. If they try something different and gutsy (while staying true to the intent of the character and the script) it will already be much more interesting than no choice at all. I always ask myself, "What is this actor bringing to the material that is original?"

—Paul Stupin
Executive Producer,
Dawson's Creek

• • •

• • •

We were auditioning for a tough and obnoxious professor on *Dawson's Creek.* One actor came in with a completely different take on the character; he played it as an aging surfer. He didn't change one line of dialogue nor did he change the intent of the character—it was an unusual interpretation and it worked. He got the job.

—Paul Stupin
Executive Producer,
Dawson's Creek

• • •

Let's keep this to ourselves (writers hate to hear it), but the fact is, *not all scripts are great.* Bear this in mind, however: Bad writing isn't wrong. It's just shallow. All you have to do is add depth to your character by making a few acting choices. There are, after all, hidden layers to any character, because there are hidden layers in all human beings. Dig up a few.

In other words, show them how the part should be played. Make strong choices. Be fully committed to your ideas. The worst that could happen is that you'll be nothing like what they want. You won't get the part. You won't get most parts, anyway; that's the business of acting. On the other hand, the best that could happen is that you'll *crystallize the role for them.* Suddenly, the character that was only partly there on paper has come alive. Now you're way ahead of the competition.

• • •

The Broadway musical *Pippin* was casting the role of the "Leading Player" (head of a band of roving players who were the theatrical framework for the story) as an *old white actor.* Due to his audition, they ended up with a *young black dancer.* (Ben Vereen, who went on to great fame because of that extraordinary performance.) He came in and, in a bravura sequence he had prepared of scene, song and dance, simply *showed them* how the part should be played.

• • •

• • •

When Courteney Cox-Arquette auditioned for *Friends*, she was right for two of the roles, Monica and Rachel, but only one appealed to her. First she read for the role she wanted (Monica), then she read for the other role (Rachel). The writer-producers liked her second audition much better, because they pictured her more in that role. When it came time to test at the network, she insisted she was better suited for the role of Monica. Although we all disagreed, the producers didn't want to lose her for both roles. We finally agreed to let her test at the network for the role of her choice, figuring if she didn't get one role, we could still offer her the other. Sure enough, she went to the network and nailed it. This doesn't happen often. In fact, it is usually the producers who end up convincing the actor. But in this case, her instincts were right. Now every week America loves her in the role she knew was best for her.

—E.K.

• • •

Don't spend too much time trying to fathom what they want. Study the material, and figure out the best way you can play the role.

After you've taken your best shot, however, the powers-that-be might give you a little input. Now you've got to suss out what it is they see in the role that they're not getting, fit that into your own ideas, and re-read. Show your flexibility, your range, and your enthusiasm for direction! We hope it doesn't come as a surprise that directors prefer to work with cooperative actors who can take direction.

Remember, *all* directors think they give good direction.

Some Hollywood directors actually do give actors good direction. You will also get direction from casting directors, writers and producers. But in film and television, actors are mostly on their own because directors often don't have the time, particularly if you have a smaller role. (A successful director once described directing as "laying down tracks in front of a speeding train.") Also, some don't have the interest and others don't have the ability. Rehearsing, in any real sense of the word, isn't often part of making films and television. At best you'll run through the scene two or three times, then wait while the director and the cinematographer light the scene and practice complicated camera tracking with the stand-ins.

That said, you may get direction at an audition. If the director gives you direction, take it. They're giving it to you for two reasons. One, they want you to be better. They like you, they're intrigued, and they want to see if you're an actor who can grow. Two, they want to know you can take direction. More specifically, that you understand them. They need to know

· · ·

Whatever you do, don't change the dialogue. Lying on your résumé pales in comparison to this sin. Never, ever, change the dialogue. Even if you hate it. Even if it is the worst dialogue you will ever utter aloud in your life. Never change the dialogue. Know it but don't change it. You never know when the writer is going to be in the room. Nothing makes us crazier. And nothing else guarantees that no matter how good you are, in fact, how truly perfect you are, you will not get the role.

—Constance Burge
**Creator of *Charmed*;
Writer for *Ed, Boston Public,
Ally McBeal***

· · ·

that you will grow in rehearsal *under their direction.*

If you are given a specific direction and you need a few moments to prepare, ask for it. Don't take too long, but don't cheat yourself either. Use common sense where time and the rhythm of an audition is concerned. Remember that, once on the set, the director will give you brief direction between takes, and you'll have to respond quickly. If you read and would like to try reading the same scene somewhat differently, you might say, "Shall I try something else?" They might be intrigued, and say, "Sure." So don't ask the question unless you have another approach to demonstrate. Better to ask, "Is there anything you'd like me to try? Anything you'd like me to do differently?"

If you get direction you don't understand, don't plow ahead. Ask for clarification. And then present them with some good, strong choices. Again (because it's important): Don't be afraid to show them how you think the part should be played. Above all, do *something* different. If you don't make an adjustment, you're just wasting everyone's time.

> • • •
>
> When I first started out in casting, one actor was extremely rude. He refused to audition for the role he was given. He was obstinate, insisting that this was obviously a mistake on my part, as the casting director never would have offended him by bringing him in to read for such a small role.
>
> When informed that there was no mistake, the actor became irate and, in front of a whole room of people, demanded to speak with the casting director. After a long discussion, the casting director let him read what he wanted. He was awful. It has been nearly ten years since that day, and that actor has just now been allowed back in my office.
>
> —Paul G. Bens, Jr.
> **Casting Director,**
> *Murder in Small Town X,*
> *Malcolm and Eddie*
> • • •

- Never change a word of the script. Even "wells" and "you knows" can madden a writer—especially in comedy, where the rhythm of the dialogue is everything.
- Don't criticize the script. That may be obvious, since the writer could be in the session, but we've seen it. Even subtle things like, "There's not much to this character, what do you want me to do?" can grate on a writer's nerves.

- Don't argue. Wait until you get the job before you get into a disagreement over how the role should be played. If you have a strong idea about that (and you should), your best bet is to play it your way first. Then, if the casting people give you another shot at it, and preface your second reading with some ideas, try to incorporate them. But to indicate in any way that what the director wants is wrong is going to shorten your career.

   So if the director wants it one way and you've planned on just the opposite, what do you do? Well, you could make a fast shift of character and play it the director's way. You'd have to be a flexible and quick actor for that. If you think you can do it, and *if* you understand what the hell he's talking about, go ahead. Or you could say, "You know, I had something else in mind for this role, do you mind if I try it that way first?" That's not at all as unusual as you might think, and it has worked with flexible directors. Of course, when you've done it your way, and they usher you quickly out of the room, don't say we recommended that approach.

There are many different kinds of acting techniques. But *how* you get there isn't really anyone's business. Not the director's (because in professional circumstances he's going to want you to deliver what he wants, and he doesn't have time for acting lessons), and least of all the audience's. What's important is *where you arrive*. Lots of things can affect the interpretation of a role. There's more than one way to play Hamlet. (Richard Burton played it a good deal differently than Mel Gibson.) The bottom line is this: You're going to have to read this role one way or the other, and if you don't choose the most comfortable, it's probably not going to be much of a reading anyway. If, after one read through, you're politely tossed out on your ear, you might console yourself with the fact that you were so far from what they wanted you probably would never have brought them around to the idea of you anyway. (Or you could console yourself by figuring the director was an idiot and missed a good thing, and save the story for your memoirs after you land a hit sitcom.) There's a maxim here that might not help you gain a role, but can increase your personal self-esteem: If you're going to fail, at least fail your way.

"May I take a moment to prepare?"

"Yes," means no. You should prepare before you come into the room, or onto the stage. You can certainly take a few seconds—a deep breath, a beat, or pause—before plunging into the first line. If the person reading with you has the first line, they may very well look at you for a nod to start. Give it to them within a few seconds. However, once the preliminaries are over, they want to hear the reading ASAP. Most directors are at best bored with, and at worst dislike, actors who turn their backs, shake out their hands, roll their heads around and generally show off their "getting into character." All that physical stuff should have been handled privately. For the reading, just take a pause, and begin.

> • • •
>
> An actor once asked me if he could have a moment to prepare and then started doing yoga for five minutes in front of the producer, director and writer. First, I had to ask the actor to go outside to finish his preparation, and then I had to beg the producers to let this guy come back in. He did not get the job.
>
> —E.K.
>
> • • •

"May I try it a different way?"

Sure. And now you better have something equally good prepared.

Try it a few different ways (as long as you ask them). Let them pick the approach they want. But in all cases, be confident and genuine.

"Do you mind if I start over?"

Well, yes, actually, they do. They are always short of time. And they may not have thought anything was wrong with your reading in the first place. (They may have thought it was going great guns. Don't be too hard on yourself.)

But this is your audition, your one chance to make a good impression. If you are thrown off by something, ask to do it again, and do it better. If you ask and are told no, accept it and move on. Starting over is okay if you've only been going for a page or two.

More than that, and it's likely they'll say, "That's okay, thanks, we've seen enough," and you won't get to start over and you don't get to finish the scene, or, they may say, "Why don't you back it up a few lines." If you really suck, get distracted, lost, whatever, and it's not too late (say you're still on the first page), go ahead and stop. They'll usually let you gather yourself together for a moment and start over. Don't take too long. And don't ask again.

Here's a decent trick if you're really lost and you're more than a page in: Stop, raise your hand to the person reading with you, take a moment, then continue where you were. That will give you a beat to pull yourself together if you think you're really going off the track, without having to start from the beginning. That little hiccup in the reading won't hurt you if they like your reading because, remember, it's not a performance, it's an audition. And they'll probably appreciate your not taking more time by starting over at the beginning.

> • • •
>
> When casting anything from one line to a series regular part, actors should come in prepared. If an actor makes a mistake I don't mind if he asks if he can do it again. But the second time he asks to start from the beginning of the scene, I start to wonder if this is how he will be on the set...
>
> —Bob Stevens
> **Writer-Creator of**
> *Crazy Love*,
> **Co-Executive Producer of**
> *Malcolm in the Middle*
> • • •

- Don't be impolite. We've already discussed this in other settings, so of course, you're not going to be rude. A chip on your shoulder will not only antagonize them, it will bring you down. Who needs that? But let's take a moment to go a little deeper here.

Their attitude could affect *you*, and sometimes, yes, *they're rude*. It happens. Power corrupts. Although the first thing we said, and the last thing we want you to remember, is that those people out there are not your enemy, and are often hoping, praying, you will be perfect for the role and their job will be satisfactorily done. But the truth is that the attitude of those people out there can sometimes be downright rude. Or just cold. Don't let it affect your audition. We don't want to be entirely Pollyanna-ish, but it's good advice, in life and in auditions, to maintain your composure as best you can under most circumstances, whether you are meeting pleasant or not-so-pleasant people. Don't let *their* rudeness make *you* hostile. If you want a career in acting, *get over it*. Also, if you can handle yourself well with a rude person in the room, the producer and casting director are likely to be impressed—it will let them know that you can probably handle a difficult director or star with equal grace.

A great many acting classes feature psychology as part of acting. Although this approach is controversial, it is sometimes unavoidable, because not everybody who wants to act is comfortable in front of others. In fact, many actors are actors because they're *uncomfortable* in front of oth-

> • • •
>
> Some years ago on Broadway, Nicol Williamson and company were about twenty minutes into *Hamlet*, when Williamson called a halt to the proceedings, admitted to the audience that he was stinking up the joint, and asked for their patience for a few minutes. Whereupon he went to his dressing room, gathered himself together, and returned to begin the *whole play from the beginning*. Legend has it the audience was mesmerized throughout and applauded wildly at the curtain.
>
> • • •

ers, and want to hide behind a role. The fact is, neurosis fuels creativity. (If you think we're going to expound on that in a small book about auditions, forget it.) So a lot of actors are neurotic, in one way or another. Successful actors use it. Those who are crippled by it are seldom successful. Suffice it to say here, there are all sorts of attitudes that can hurt an actor at an audition, and we don't mean just the chip-on-the-shoulder, or the I'm-too-good-for-this-role, or the you-should-be-auditioning-for-me categories. Also avoid these unproductive attitudes:

- "I'm not good enough."
- "I'm worthless."
- "I hope I don't get this job, because then I'll have to come up with the goods."
- "I'm the child, they're the parents."

None of these will help you demonstrate your abilities, and certainly not your confidence. Of course, most people with such mental blocks don't always know it. Before you begin to undertake the seemingly endless rounds of auditions and rejections that are the lot of the actor, closely and honestly examine your feelings about it, and deal with them. Somehow, you've got to make your feelings work for you. Character is destiny.

Most common of all is the fear factor. Nerves can be crippling to an actor. In fact, most actors feel that auditions are more nerve-racking than performances, probably because they're more prepared for a performance. (Which, of course, is why you should be well prepared for an audition.) We could tell you, don't be nervous. But what good would that do? Besides the usual—preparation, warm-up, visualizing your success—the single most valuable tool to overcome nervousness is *concentration*. On the role, and on the job at hand. If you're thinking, *God, I really need this job*, it's going to distract you.

Use your nervousness to your advantage. Concentrate that nervous energy, and "Never let them see you sweat." If that doesn't work, try this: You *are* going to make a fool of yourself. So what? That's what acting really is.

• • •

I've auditioned actors at many levels in television—beginners, co-stars, guest stars, actors who have starred on their own sitcoms—believe me when I say this: *Actors at all levels are nervous when they audition*.

—Bob Stevens
Writer-Creator of
Crazy Love,
Co-Executive Producer of
Malcolm in the Middle

• • •

In Short...

You are auditioning from the moment you walk in the door, until the moment you walk out of the door.

- Don't be late, obnoxious, or impatient.
- Don't forget the sides you were given.
- Don't memorize the lines so well that you become inflexible.
- Don't be timid with your approach to the role.
- Don't wear distracting clothing, or cover your face with your hair.
- Don't audition for something you definitely would not do, or are not available for.
- Don't be self-deprecating.
- Don't ask the casting director if you have a callback.

. . . .

- Do show them how the part should be played.
- Do dress the part.
- Do use common sense and common courtesy.

12

Taping Auditions

Many auditions videotape the actors, so the director and producers, who may not be present, can review them at a later date. Almost all commercial calls do this. Though you should be warned in advance, don't let it throw you if they spring this on you. Although women might want to take a little more time with their makeup, this is not a "screen test," and you won't be pampered by a crew. Usually an assistant will just shoot your reading with a camcorder.

- Ask questions to make sure you understand the parameters of the taping. Do they want you to look straight into the camera? Focus on a particular off-camera spot? Before you begin, know if you should stand up or sit down, and how much you can move around. If they're going to do this all day, they've got a routine pretty well set.
- They will probably ask you to state your name, the role, and possibly your agency. When slating, relax. It's easier to say, "My name is Richard Burton—I'm repped by the Mojo Talent Agency," than it is to blurt out, "Richard Burton, Mojo Talent." It also gives you a chance to show a little more personality up front. Go with what's comfortable.
- If you are supposed to look directly into the camera—as in many commercial auditions—imagine the camera is your

beloved grandmother, or a close friend. Or maybe your shrink. Someone specific. Anything but a mass audience. This will help you be more intimate, which is key to screen acting.

- Don't project to a camera, ever. No matter how far away the camera is, be natural. The operator may have zoomed in. In fact, don't project at any audition, unless it's on a stage, or for the theatre. Most of the Hollywood rooms you'll audition in will be small, with the casting people just across the room, if not closer. Projecting, of course, is only the tip of the iceberg where the difference between film, television and stage acting are concerned. If you're unclear of the difference, go to an on-camera acting class or workshop.
- Don't whisper, either. Especially if you are being taped. The microphone won't be good enough to pick up your voice.
- Don't worry that you're not doing enough. It's true that the proverbial raised eyebrow is forty feet tall on the screen, and that means almost any expression beyond the realistic should be confined to the stage. ("Stage" can mean sitcoms as well. Sitcom actors sometimes seem to be shouting at each other, as if they were performing for a live audience, which they often are.)

• • •

When in doubt, don't shout. When I worked on David E. Kelley's *Boston Public*, the casting director, Laura Schiff, welcomed the writer-producers to all of the casting sessions. And usually, the writer of the soon-to-be-filming episode would join the other two producers in the room. Because *Boston Public* centered around a high school, most of the actors who were auditioning were auditioning for the role of various high school students. Which means that most of them were young and fairly green. Still, nothing screamed "amateur" more than the actors who would come in and literally yell their lines at us. Why, I have no idea, I just know that any actor who ever did this never got the role. So save your yelling for sporting events.

—Constance Burge
**Creator of *Charmed*; Writer for *Ed*,
Boston Public, *Ally McBeal***

• • •

- Underplay or overplay? For film and television, underplay is always better. The best generic direction ever given in film is, "Do nothing." The camera is an amazing tool. It catches everything. If you think it, it will be there.

In Short...

- Don't project to the camera.

....

- Do ask how much room you have to move around when being taped.

13

Auditions for Actors

Acting is not the province of this book. If you aren't yet comfortable acting, don't go on auditions until you are.

However, we want to warn you about a few more things you can succumb to at auditions, and to do so, we're going to need some ground rules. Here's a simple one for actors:

- Act verbs, not nouns. That is shorthand for the fact that it's easier to *do something* than to *be someone*. Or, put another way, you're not likely to get good results *being* a character directly. But if you *do things* the character would do (and say things the character would say, but that's up to the writer), then the character is going to be clear to the audience. (That is, if you're doing it with believability and commitment.) After all, we identify people by their words and actions.

    That's not to say there aren't *characteristics* you may want to include. A mad scientist might not have his hair perfectly groomed. A sexy woman will be sexier in high heels. An anal retentive will have neatly pressed clothes. Someone insecure might not look right at people. You'll choose appropriate indications of who you are playing from your posture to your mannerisms.

But it's hard to play the "handsome, charming but conceited man" who "enters the room." (That's also bad screenwriting, but you'll see it in scripts quite often.) That's hard to act, because handsome and charming and conceited are descriptions. But when you read that, you can think to yourself, "I'm God's gift to women, just wait until they get a load of me in there," as you enter, and maybe it will work. Perhaps try to find a subtle piece of business to suggest your character's personality. In the example, the actor might preen a bit, running his hand over his hair (just once—remember, you're going for *subtle*). Translate *description* into *intention* and *action* where you can.

- Make sure the intention is accurate. Actors try to cry; people are usually trying *not* to cry.

Inexperienced actors playing a drunk scene will slur their words, stumble around, and in various ways try to act drunk. But what any good actor knows is that drunks usually *don't want you to know they're drunk.* (For an excellent example of this, see Gene Hackman's performance in *Absolute Power.*) They're trying to keep it together. Not trying to stumble, but trying to walk straight. Not trying to slur their words, but to enunciate clearly. If you have to play a scene drunk—one of the most difficult acting exercises

• • •

My favorite audition story is when I auditioned for *Hill Street Blues*. The character was an older woman who was being left by her younger lover and the situation called for tears, which I just could not seem to get to happen in my preparation. I thought about it for a while and decided that although I couldn't muster tears for the lover leaving, if I thought about my kids leaving, I would definitely cry. I mean, tears are tears, right? Actually, not really. I finished the audition and the producer asked me if I would try it again. He said, "This seems more like your kids are leaving than your lover." Wow, what a demonstration of what is in your mind showing on your face!

—K Callan
Actress and Author

• • •

there is—you're not going to get very far just trying to *be drunk*, because the true drunk is trying *not to be drunk*. Prepare with this understanding: Alcohol restricts normal social inhibitors. It releases people to say or do what they have repressed.

When playing a scene, the key is to figure what the character *really* wants to do or say before you make your choices.

- Be specific. Specifics are much more effective than generalities. You'll want to know as much as you can about the character, then choose the actions and intentions that will identify that character to the audience. You might come across a character who is shy. *How* a shy person acts and reacts in the situation is the key to presenting the character. You might come across an adult character who was abused as a child. *How* an abused child might react as an adult in certain situations is the key to presenting that character.

In other words, do not try to play the *quality* of the character, but rather, seek and play the way the character would *express* that quality.

The difficulty is this: There can be a whole lot of people at auditions who might find it necessary to give you direction—ad agency representatives, sponsors, stage managers, producers, casting directors—who really haven't much of a background in the theory of acting. They're going to say things to you like, "Be bigger," "Be broader," and our personal favorite, "Have fun with it!" Don't just try to be bigger or broader. (And we've never understood how to "have fun" with something.) Quickly translate these instructions into something you can *do*. Get angrier at the situation your character is in. Decide that this particular underarm deodorant is exactly what you've been looking for, and be grateful when you apply it. Don't just giggle for the sake of giggling. (Laughing being, perhaps, the second hardest acting assignment.) Find something very funny in the scene to react to.

- Along these lines, don't try to play your own type either. "Sexy," "Cute," "Hunky" may be in the breakdown, but words like that can mislead you. If the breakdown said, "good-looking, 40-year-old female," and your agent sent your picture and résumé in, and you got a call, there's no harm in making sure you're not having a bad hair day when you hit the mirror in the morning, but when you get there, *play the role, not the type.*

- Don't give a boring audition, and fall back on the excuse that the character was weak. There are no weak characters. There are people, however, who want to do more, to be more, to say more than they do, but they are repressed or inhibited.

- Good actors *listen.* If the other character in the scene—even if it's being read in a monotone by a stage manager or casting director behind the table—is talking, listen and react. The old adage is true: Acting is reacting.

• • •

There was an actor who auditioned for a small role on *Charmed*. He looked the part and he nailed the audition. Everyone in the room agreed he was perfect. There was just one small problem: Politics of the business dictated that the part had to go to someone else. In a perfect world, I would have called the agent, explained the situation, and the agent could then call the actor and let him know what had happened. Then again, in a perfect world, he would have been given the part.... Anyway, I couldn't call the agent, but I remembered this actor and I created a role specifically for him later in the season. It was actually a much better part than the one he had originally auditioned for, which meant a better credit, more screen time, and a lot more money. The point of this story—and I promise, there is one—is that I'm willing to bet you know when you've nailed an audition, too. You know when you're right for a part, when you're prepared for a part, and when the people in the room love you. So when you don't get a job that you thought for sure was going to be coming your way, try not to take it personally. Something better just may be headed your way in the very near future.

—Constance Burge
Creator of *Charmed*; Writer for *Ed*,
Boston Public*, *Ally McBeal

• • •

- Frank Loesser had a sign in his office that read, "Loud is good, big is better." Actors today might do well to paraphrase that with, "Truth is good, big truth is better."

This book isn't meant to teach you how to act. There are many good (and bad) acting teachers out there. There are universities with great theatre programs. (Hint: You're not going to learn to act in the film department.) There are even conservatories where you can indulge in every aspect of the theatre without having to take a biology class at the same time. There are various codified methods, from The Method to the more classical traditions. We won't discuss the panorama of approaches, it's not our business. And we mean this literally. You see...

The director *doesn't care how you do it, so long as you deliver the goods.*

If you're doing a scene in an acting class or workshop, it will be developed organically from the acting work you've been doing. You won't have to audition, and the teacher directing the scene will coach you into playing the role effectively.

If you think you're going to be pampered like that on the job, you've got a surprise coming.

In the business of acting, it's a director's job to pull together the various elements of a stage or screen production, and the characters delivering the story are only one small part of that. Actors who receive any useful direction at all will be hearing *what the director wants,* not *how the director thinks you should get there.* You're going to have to arrive at that emotion or action on your own.

. . .

I have always had good feelings for actors who come in prepared—some dress the part, but nothing too distracting; some bring props, but nothing that takes over the scene. With these performers, I look forward to their auditions. They get my undivided attention, no matter how rushed the session may be.

—Lloyd Segan
Executive Producer,
The Dead Zone

. . .

Of course you've prepared. You've taken acting classes, and you know how to approach a role. If you've gotten a good look at the whole script or the sides some days in advance, then you've practiced out loud at least enough to settle on an approach. If you're going in for a cold reading—getting handed the material when you arrive, and being allowed only a few minutes to look it over—you're going with the confidence that *you'll think of something*. In the latter case, don't panic. After all, some of the best artistic choices arrive because of the chances one takes on one's intuition when one doesn't have too much time to brood over all the available avenues.

In order to do this, you sometimes have to...

FILL IN THE BLANKS

When you have very little idea about the full script you're going to have to fill in a great deal. Sometimes there isn't a script, as in the case of an audition for a commercial, which is going to show only a slice of life. Assess the situation you're in. For example, you might have to sit at a table eating a new food product for a commercial. Probably they haven't given too much thought—or anyway haven't told you—what's going on around you. Make something up. Is it breakfast, lunch, or dinner? Is someone else in the room? What room? How hungry are you? Why? Do you like the food? (Of course you do! It's the sponsor's product!) There's nothing mysterious about this, and it should be basic to your rehearsal process, whether weeks in a studio for a Chekhov play, or a few moments to yourself in a waiting room before a pre-read. Imagine a more complete setting than what it may say in the script. Know where you are. Imagine what the people you're talking to look like. (Probably not like the casting director who is reading your cues.) Then you'll have something to react to, something you can play. These things may not be evident, may not come across, but they will support your work. Particularly in auditions, this is a quick way to get a fuller sense of reality and believability in your work.

A WORD ABOUT COMEDY

Don't try to be funny. Every good comedic performance starts with the actor playing the heart of the character. If the writing is there, all you have to do is play it. You will want to find some larger-than-life moments. Seeing a sad sack slip on a banana peel is funny to us only if the sad sack doesn't see it coming (or the villain deserves it, or the uptight woman has her arrogance punctured), but never if the actor tries to be funny. You can "make a bit" out of a moment if you're embellishing it, but you have to do it with the proper motivation. Find something to react to that your character would generally find startling, and you can double-take all you want. Without the motivation, it will feel forced and futile.

THE MONOLOGUE

If you're an actor, you must have at least two monologues you are prepared to perform at the drop of a prop hat. Many theatre directors will want to see one or both. Many regional theatres will want to see monologues. For film and television, monologues are less common, but still necessary. For a "general"—an audition in which the casting director is just meeting actors for their general files—a monologue can be very useful.

You need at least two, because you need one classical and one contemporary, one comedic and one dramatic. (Okay, that sounds like four. But you can figure that out.) There's an unlimited amount of dramatic literature out there, so there's no excuse for not finding two great pieces that suit you. There are lots of anthologies of monologues. (If you find one you like from a monologue book, don't just learn it from the book. Go get the play or film and study the whole arc of the character.) You can adapt things from novels. You can look to screenplays as well as plays or musicals. You can also create a monologue out of several shorter speeches from a play by skipping the other character's responses. If you've already played a role that featured a monologue, that would certainly give you a leg up on the character.

There are two styles of monologue. The outer monologue, in which you are ranting to another character on stage, and the inner monologue, better known as the soliloquy. Perform both the way you would on stage. For the outer monologue, you'll have to "place" the character or characters you are speaking to. You can use a chair, which should help you focus, or just place them in a certain space. (Downstage! Don't upstage yourself with an imaginary character.) You'll want to make it clear where they are by focusing on them from time to time, but it is not necessary to look at the space you've chosen all the time. You'll notice—because as an actor you've surreptitiously observed people in real life situations—that people talking often don't make much eye contact. In a monologue, you can use that to your advantage by moving away, physically and visually, from your intended spot of focus, and back to it, as the material suggests.

For the inner monologue, or soliloquy, you'll be talking to yourself. Not as easy, but not as difficult as it seems, if you just remember that in real life, people talk to themselves all the time. Maybe not out loud. Maybe their lips don't move. But they do it. All you need to do is physicalize it.

A few hints on monologues:

- Don't do anything so popular everyone knows it (especially the director, who may have his own ideas about the proper interpretation). That probably eliminates "To be or not to be."
- Don't do anything from a role you couldn't play on the stage. Teenagers should not be playing King Lear just yet.
- For general film and television auditions, use a contemporary monologue, playing a role you could be realistically cast for.
- For film and television, go ahead and do something from film or television if you like. Or from a play. Keep in mind the genre you may be auditioning for. If the casting director does a lot of sitcoms, do something comedic.
- For theatre, do something from a play. Big and bravura, theatrical, with language as music.
- Don't make eye contact with the casting people. Personally we don't mind, but some people don't like being a part of the scene. It makes them uncomfortable, and they won't be able to evaluate your performance.
- Don't go it alone on this, it's too important. Take it to your acting teacher or coach to help you prepare.

SHAKESPEARE

This is the best and the worst of challenges for an actor. The best, because his writing is so fluid, his characters so rich, and his canon so full of great monologues and soliloquies. The worst, because he's so bloody difficult to do. If you're going to do a Shakespearean monologue, you'd better have good diction, a great speaking voice, and a real sense of what the full character is about. Study the whole play, not just the monologue you copied out of a book of monologues.

There are many ways to play Shakespeare, of course, but in general, an actor today is much better off ignoring the iambic pentameter rhythm, the rhymes and the scansion, and delivering the sentences more realistically. Realism replaced declamation in the theatre more than a hundred years ago. You'll seem much more believable if you get past the poetry and focus on character. The great poetry will be there anyway. Don't play it. Play the character and what he or she has to say. It's a good idea to type out the scene in the normal fashion of contemporary dialogue, ignoring the lines of the original folio that are featured in all published editions. This will help you get to the true meaning of the sentences.

ON A STAGE VS. IN A ROOM

The difference between auditioning on stage (usually for theatre) and auditioning in a room (usually for film or television) is one of degree. If you're on a stage, *project!* If you're not, don't. (If you're in a room, but auditioning for the theatre, go ahead and shake the walls. That's what theatre people are looking for.)

A little training should enable a good actor to do this. The difficulty comes when you've been away from it for awhile. British actors have it easy. With London the center of all entertainment activity, they are constantly performing in all mediums. Americans, who have to choose between New York and Hollywood, can, if they live in Hollywood, go years without performing on the stage. We have seen very good actors who live in Hollywood fly to New York for a theatre audition, only to fail miserably on a stage. At the same time, we have seen theatre actors who fly to Hollywood for pilot season play to the balcony, and they're not helping themselves either. Adjust.

In Short...

- Don't try to play a character's characteristics. Play his intentions and actions.

- Don't prepare a monologue for a role you couldn't play.

- Don't fail to adjust your technique to the physical circumstances—don't project in a room, don't mumble on a stage.

14

Auditions for Singers

More supplicants show up at a call for singers for a Broadway musical than any other category. Singing—in shows, on records, in nightclubs—is a tough corner of the business, with thousands of applicants for every job. It sometimes appears as if everyone thinks they can sing.

If you're trying out for the chorus, you'll most likely be asked to sing the proverbial "sixteen bars," after which you'll get a "thank you," or be asked to hang around. If you're up for a role, you'll probably be singing a full chorus of a song you have prepared, then something from the show's score if you're under serious consideration. Either way, give yourself the best chance. A few pointers:

- Warm-up before you go. At the theatre or rehearsal hall there usually isn't much extra space, and you can't belt out your ma-me-mo's in the wings or the hallway while another singer is taking his turn. Los Angeles singers have it easy, they can sing in the car, along with the radio or karaoke tapes during the drive. Taxi drivers in New York are used to people vocalizing in their back seats. If you have to take the subway to your audition, better get up early and warm up the pipes before you leave.
- Don't go to auditions out of good vocal condition. Someone important might hear you at your worst. Here's a famous

opera singer's anecdote: "If I don't practice one day, I can tell. If I don't practice two days, my wife can tell. If I don't practice three days, the audience can tell."

- Don't let your patience or your energy desert you. We've seen long, long lines of applicants at chorus calls or general auditions. It is certainly debilitating to arrive at 9:00 a.m. and not get to sing until 1:00 p.m. This probably holds true for anyone auditioning anything anywhere: You've got to stay focused. Move around when you need to, don't sit in one place too long, try to relax, but above all, keep that natural energy that comes from a tense situation in control, without losing its benefits. Meditation, anyone?

- Don't sing Avril Lavigne if they're asking for a Broadway standard. If they're asking for something contemporary, don't sing Rodgers and Hart. If you can ascertain precisely the nature of the show you are auditioning for, go ahead and target it. By all means, try to have your agent find out what their parameters are, or ask when you get there. Be prepared by having learned a number of songs in different styles and genres, and carry your favorites with you.

  Sometimes the answer to "What do you want to hear?" will be, "Sing whatever shows off your voice the best." Do it. Don't try to outguess them, just pick a song that shows off your voice to its best advantage. If you still don't know what to sing, you haven't taken enough voice lessons yet.

  Musical comedy singers used to be prepared with both "an up-tempo" and "a ballad." Then along came *Jesus Christ Superstar*, and everyone had to have a "contemporary" in their repertoire as well as a "legit."

  If they do have a request, don't ignore it. Not only are you wasting their time singing an opera aria when they wanted the Beatles, but you're *not following instructions*, and they hate that.

- Don't sing a song by a living composer if the composer is sitting out there in the dark auditioning you for his latest show. It's too great a risk. Some composers love to hear their own songs. Most, however, will warn you to stay away from their catalogue, because they've heard their own stuff too many times by too many good people, and you risk falling short. Moreover, they know exactly how they want their song phrased, and if you miss by as much as an eighth-note, they could be annoyed. If you're not sure which ego you're auditioning for, don't tempt it.

- Don't sing a very, very popular song. Shortly after the film version of *Cabaret* came out, one out of every two female singers on Broadway was auditioning with "Maybe This Time." Why compete with a dozen other singers who went before you? Why compete with Liza Minnelli? If a certain song is currently very popular at auditions, stay away from it. There's nothing more deflating than standing in the wings, your turn next, and hearing someone sing the very song you're clutching in your sweaty palms. (Unless it's hearing them sing it really well. That's worse.)

- Similarly, don't sing a song that's too familiar. Pick something that everyone knows well and you'll be fighting the version they like best. Fall short, and they're not going to be complimentary. Which brings us to singing "People." Unless you really believe you're going to sing it better than Barbra Streisand did—and if you do, you're deluded—don't sing it. Don't sing a song that is overly identified with one particular star in one particular version, because the chances are you're not going to be better than they are. Which leaves only one possibility—to be worse. Being the second best singer of Jule Styne's "People" is not chopped liver, but it's going to be a subconscious strike against you. Why risk it? The exception: If you have a truly unique version that is so different from the original it stands on its own, then okay. A man might sing "People" for instance (though we don't recommend it).

- Don't sing a song that's too unfamiliar, either. If you sing something too unique, such as special material written just for your nightclub act, or an obscure song from an obscure show from an obscure decade, you can draw too much attention to the song, and not enough to your voice.

    Of course, there is an exception to this rule. (Didn't we tell you there are exceptions to every rule?) Use your common sense and, if you have a good reason to do something unorthodox, do it. If the quality of your voice is less important than your performance, then special material, material you can act, might be more in your line. In that case, make it unique, and sell it.

In general, try to choose material somewhere in the middle. Not so popular that you're going to be the ninth person to sing it today, not so unique that it draws a lot of attention away from your voice.

- Sing something that flatters you. Don't overestimate your range. Of course, you've practiced the song a hundred times, so it should sit comfortably on your voice, even if you've had to alter the key.
- Don't bring sheet music in E-flat and tell the piano player to play it in D-flat. Why take the chance that the piano player they've hired isn't good at transposing, and gums up your accompaniment? If you want to do a song in an unpublished key, ask your vocal coach to write out the chords on the music in advance.
- Don't sing a song whose context doesn't suit you. Ten-year-olds trying out for *Annie* should not sing, "It cost me a lot, but there's one thing that I've got, it's my man..."
- Make sure you can identify with the lyrics. Here's a tip directly from Jule Styne himself, composer of *Gypsy, Funny Girl, Peter Pan, Bells Are Ringing* and many, many more: "The great singers sing the lyrics, not the melody." (And this from the guy who wrote the music, not the words!)

  You're going to be on pitch (or your voice teacher is stealing your money). The quality of your voice should come naturally (or you need a new voice teacher), albeit subtly enhanced with good breathing technique and placement. And we're not talking opera singing, in which tone is all and context is nearly irrelevant. In popular singing, which we define as anything from "Come Pick the Flowers in My Garden, Maud" to the golden age of Broadway musicals to "Sk8er Boi," what's going to put over the song is your *delivery of the text*. Pick a song you can identify with, and sing it like you mean it. Deliver the thoughts with commitment.
- Don't do a lot of choreography. They want to hear you sing, not see you dance. Racing around the stage and doing back-flips off the proscenium arch (saw it once) should be

saved for those times you're absolutely sure that's what they're looking for.

On the other hand, don't stand there stiff as a board, either. Relax (ha!), enjoy the song, let your body do what it would naturally do in performance, but without choreography.

- Don't sing a long song. If they liked your sixteen bars well enough to call you back for more, thirty-two bars is all they want to hear. Many composers are too polite, and won't ever cut you off, but they'll lose interest, even talk among themselves. Others are more than happy to wave their hand in the middle of your high note and shout, "Thank you!" as soon as they've made a decision. Don't give them the chance. Yes, this cuts out "Soliloquy" from *Carousel*, and "Molasses to Rum to Slaves" from *1776*. Often actors want to do songs like that, because they've prepared various moods and bits, and want to show they can put over a song in character. Good idea, but do it with a shorter song.

"Do you mind if I start over?"

Yes they do. It's usually a long day for people out there sitting through singing auditions. They're more comfortable when things are moving along nicely. Don't stop, realize you're not giving your best performance, and ask the piano player to take it from the top, unless you've just started, and you are already lost. If you forget the lyrics, hum along, yada yada, make 'em laugh, and look at the piano player with pleading eyes. If he's hip to the scene, he'll throw you a lyric. Try to give the powers that be the impression that, lost as you may be, you're confident enough to bowl on through until you can get back on track. After all, that's what you'd have to do in performance.

- Don't blame the piano player. Even something subtle like, "Sorry, I usually have my own accompanist," isn't very polite. They're going to see you as either a complainer or an excuser, two performer types directors would prefer not to work with (and you've made an enemy of the piano player for life).

- If you're called back for another, further audition, or just asked to hang around until the first round of eliminations are over, and then asked to sing again, don't change clothes and don't change songs. Sing the same song that impressed them the first time. They've seen a lot of people, and may forget why they asked you back. They need to be reminded. Especially if it's weeks later. If you sang sixteen bars, they may want to hear the entire song. Eventually they'll ask you to sing something else. That's your chance to expand on your repertoire. If they make specific requests, try your best to satisfy them. "We're looking for a soprano, what's your highest note?" or "We're doing _Grease_ this summer, do you have anything from that period?" are the kinds of things you might hear, and you'll want to be prepared. Have a repertoire.
- They may want to see you dance. Even if you're not a dancer, throw yourself into it as best you can. Musicals need _characters_, and not everybody needs to be Fred Astaire.
- Finally, don't ask everyone on your way out, "How was I?" Hold your head up, even if you cracked on that high note, and smile. There's always acting.

In Short...

- Don't fail to follow instructions—sixteen bars is sixteen bars.

. . . .

- Do prepare several songs in different styles.

15

Auditions for Dancers

Two of the greatest choreographers of the golden age of Broadway musicals were Jerome Robbins and Bob Fosse. When Bob Fosse held an audition, his first speech was encouraging: "I want to thank you for coming. I know auditioning is a difficult process, I wish I could hire all of you. If I eliminate you today, don't hesitate to come back next time and try again." When Jerome Robbins held an audition, his opening remarks to the gathered dancers went something like this: "This is a difficult show. You have to be technically proficient. If you're not, don't waste my time, and don't embarrass yourself. Leave now." The temperature dipped several degrees. That's two very different introductions for nervous young dancers dying to be in a Broadway musical.

I guess the moral here is, don't lose your cool. Try to enjoy an audition, no matter how frightening the production people might be. Choreographers can be very scary indeed. There's a kind of sadomasochism built into the world of dance as it is.

That said, of all the auditions in show business, dancing probably is the most fun. Though no less nerve-racking, at least you get to dance a good bit and, if the choreographer and the stage manager are reasonably efficient, you get a fair amount of time on the stage or in the rehearsal room, because dance auditions can be done in large groups. Usually the choreographer teaches everyone

• • •

Fosse...had them do a big jump combination across the stage, a combination that ended in a double pirouette. As each girl finished, Fosse would say, "Stay," or, "I'm sorry, thank you." One very nervous girl did her preparation and then executed the steps with a frozen smile on her face. When she finished, she turned expectantly to Fosse; he very nicely said, "Thank you. I'm sorry." Apparently this was not the reaction she had been expecting. She picked up her large dance bag, walked up to Fosse, who was sitting on a stool at the front of the stage, and hit him so hard with the bag, she knocked him clean off the stool. "Nobody says *I'm sorry* to me!" she screamed. Both stage managers rushed in to take her away. Fosse brushed himself off, smoothed back his hair, and said, "Ladies, no more dance bags on stage."

—from *Bob Fosse's Broadway* by Margery Beddow

• • •

the routine at once—though sometimes so many dancers show up that even on the stage of a Broadway musical house the stage manager has to split applicants into fifty or so at a time—and then, when he is satisfied that everyone has had a chance to learn it, asks the dancers to perform the routine two or three at a time. Then he eliminates, asking some dancers to stay, nodding a polite "thank you" to the others.

- Don't show up out of shape, or with rusty technique. When employed and working in a show night after night, you're going to do repetitive routines, only using certain muscles and certain techniques. Continue to take class every day to keep your overall technique sharp. For that matter, if you're not a dancer who loves to take dance classes every day, it's not a career for you. Here are two good reasons to take class:

    One, when you're not taking class, be aware that someone else is, and when you go to the next audition, they're going to be there too.

    Two, in a few years, when you're barely middle-aged and still have a whole life in front of you, your dance career is going to be over. Which days will you look back upon with satisfaction—the ones you were dancing, or the ones when you slept late?

- Don't arrive at the last minute. Arrive early. This is more important for dancers than anyone else, because many choreographers will not give you the opportunity to warm up. They'll arrive on time, teach you the first routine, then ask you to perform it for them. Once, twice if you're lucky. Then they start eliminating.

  On the West Coast, where the weather is warm, dress is casual, and you drive to an audition in your car, a lot of dancers come ready to dance. On the East Coast, where it's cold and you're probably taking the subway, it's more traditional to bring a dance bag filled with dance clothes, and change in dressing rooms or in the basement of the theatre. Whatever you do, allow for the time it takes to get dressed and warm up properly. Even in California, avoid the laid-back California approach to the clock when you are going to a dance audition. Choreographers, because of the discipline of their profession, can be particularly annoyed with latecomers.

- Don't wear overly revealing clothes. Okay, all dance clothes are pretty revealing, and yes, don't wear clothes that hide your shape. It's your shape that you're selling. (Many classic ballet teachers want to see your line, and won't even allow sweatpants and sweatshirts in class once the barré is complete, even on a cold day.) But going to a legitimate audition in an outfit designed for the stage of the Club Pussycat isn't professional. Even topless dancers in Las Vegas don't dance the audition routine topless. (The ones who make it through the dance audition are then asked to pull down their leotards while the choreographer and his assistants make notes.)

  Regarding nudity: If you're not in a completely professional situation, with several other dancers present, preferably governed by a performer's union, don't fall for it. Even the classic erotic review *Oh! Calcutta!* didn't ask to see the whole package until the finals, and an Equity representative had to be present.

  In fact, we'd say that anything too flashy—spangled or mesh tights, Bali Hai blouses—distracts from *you* and *your technique*. Wear normal dance clothes, preferably in solid colors. Girls wear tights and leotards. Boys, do not wear tights and leotards except to a ballet audition. If there's one thing that can set a good male dancer apart from the crowd, it's *masculinity*. Nobody gives a damn about your sexual preferences, but if there's anything that can kill a male dancer's career, it's looking effeminate on stage. While classical dance companies will want you in tights, for musicals and music videos you're better off in dance pants.

An exception: hip-hop dancers. Lots of video choreographers these days are working in contemporary styles. If you're sure that is all the audition is going to consist of—and you're not going to be asked to demonstrate pas de bourrés and grand jétes—go ahead and dress appropriately. (Though how the great breakers dance in hugely oversized clothes is a mystery.)

- Many choreographers have "audition" routines they like to use first, to eliminate any dancers who are clearly undertrained, or the wrong type for their show. This first routine might be simple, but the choreographer is looking to see if you have a solid foundation, which usually means ballet technique, even if there isn't any classical dancing in the show. Jack Cole used to ask for eight grand *battéments* forward and eight back, then single, double and triple *pirouettes*, alternating sides. Agnes de Mille often wanted to see *grandé jêtes* across the floor. Bob Fosse's was the most famous. His "Tea For Two" routine was a deceptively simple, graceful jazz combination, but it showed line, height on a jump, turns and style all at once. You can see it in his autobiographical film *All That Jazz*, in the opening sequence, though he used the song "On Broadway" instead of the classic soft-shoe song he had used throughout his career.

  If you hear about this routine, for goodness sake give yourself a head start and learn it before you arrive. Any dancers who have already auditioned for that choreographer will know it. After Michael Bennett had created *A Chorus Line*, he was looking to cast two more companies as well as understudies and replacements on Broadway. He used the jazz routine and the ballet routine from the opening number for the show's subsequent auditions. Word got out, and dancers all over New York were learning it, teaching it to each other, and practicing it, weeks before the auditions.

- Don't show up with only one pair of shoes. Heels break. Laces break. Leather splits. Different floors can require different traction. If this is your big break, be prepared. Girls should carry at least both flats and heels. If you're not sure what kind of choreography the audition is going to consist of, don't hesitate to ask the choreographer or his assistant when you get there, then put on appropriate shoes. Flat shoes save a lot of wear and tear on the calves and knees of girl dancers, but choreographers don't care about your health, they care about what you look like, and a lot of choreography is eventually going to be performed in stylish shoes. The fact is, the female leg looks a lot sexier in heels. If you can tap dance, bring tap shoes. (Unless, of course, you're sure that there isn't going to be any tap in the audition. For a tour of *Fiddler on the Roof*, you won't need them, we promise.)

- Speaking of tap, don't leave any of the basic dance styles out of your dance education. For one thing, they all influence each other. (You can spot a ballet dancer with no tap training right away, because they usually have an insufficient sense of rhythm.) Go to a few flamenco classes, a few belly dancing classes, a few of just-about-anything-you-can-find classes, to familiarize yourself with the basics in every style. It's fun, and in musicals in particular, you never know what you'll need.

- Don't deviate from the choreography. Don't do three pirouettes when the choreographer has asked for two. Don't jump so high that you come down later than the count the choreographer has given you. Choreographers want to see what they have choreographed *exactly* as they choreographed it.

- Don't chitchat with other dancers who you worked with two years ago and haven't seen since. Catch up with show biz gossip on your own time. For your own sake, focus all your energy and attention on the audition, because choreographers are the most demanding of your time of all directors. While you're warming up, concentrate on making that transition from the busy streets, hectic traffic, agent phone calls and acting classes to the circumstances before you. Learn the steps. Go over and over them. Watch how the other dancers perform them. When you're relegated to the side to wait your turn, don't talk to your neighbors. Watch the other dancers, listen to the music, feel the steps in your body, keep your energy going, and focus on the music and the choreography until it's your turn to perform for the choreographer. *Visualize* how well you're going to do it when it's your turn.

- When you do get the chance, *smile.* Throughout this book, we've been talking about *confidence*, and how it makes you stand out. Dance is no different. Aside from the obvious fact that a nervous dancer is a shaky dancer whose turns are going to wobble and whose jumps are going to crash land, if you don't *command the stage* with your body, you're not going to look much like a great dancer.

  Okay, you shouldn't necessarily smile all the time. It depends on the choreography you are executing. You don't want to be performing steps for the rumble in *West Side Story* as if you were ushering Dolly Levi around the runway in *Hello, Dolly!* If you're auditioning for an existing show, know the show. If you aren't sure what you are auditioning for, listen to the music, watch the choreographer and his assistants, and feel the mood. Then project it.

- Don't look like you're looking at yourself in the mirror, don't look like you're trying to remember the steps, and don't look down at the floor as if the steps were written there. This last rule is a *Don't* so common it was written into the opening audition scene in *A Chorus Line* as "Boy in the headband." ("Look up!")

- Here's a helpful hint for your class work: Be sure to perform class routines facing *away* from the mirror at least a few times. Dance classrooms are outfitted with floor to ceiling mirrors. Classes are conducted with the students looking at themselves in those mirrors. That mirror has a tendency to become, by the teenage years, a crutch. Inexperienced dancers often find themselves performing with much less bravura, with, even, a timidity and complete lack of confidence, when they suddenly find themselves without it. Avoiding this is simple. At the end of every class, whatever routine you have been working on should be performed facing away from the mirror at least a couple of times.

- If you're given a callback, go over the original routine the night before, because it's very likely the audition will at least begin with what you learned the first time around. Be prepared for some new routines, too. And in some cases, if you're looking for a chorus job in a musical, there will be much more. So...

- Don't show up without your sheet music. For a lot of shows, dancers have to sing too. Check out Chapter 18, and be just as prepared as the singers are with a legit song, a contemporary song, a comic song, sixteen bars, etc. If you're tone deaf, go to a good musical comedy vocal coach and come up with a song that anyone can sing. Show them you can at least do the Rex Harrison thing—the talking on pitch that made him triumphant in *My Fair Lady*—and that you're willing to blast along with the rest of them if you have to.

- Finally, don't show up without a résumé (see Chapter 3). Just because you're only auditioning for the chorus doesn't mean the choreographer isn't interested in your background— where you studied, who you've worked for. And a smart director is helping the choreographer choose the chorus, because he knows he's going to have to pull his understudies from there. Sutton Foster, the star of *Thoroughly Modern Millie*, was recast from the chorus line to the title role, and won a Tony for her work. Who knows, you may be going out there a chorus girl, but you could be coming back a star.

In Short...

- Don't ever stop going to class.
- Don't change the choreography.
- Don't show up without something to sing.

. . . .

- Do arrive in plenty of time to warm up.

16

The Callback

Sometimes after a pre-read, you'll be asked to wait for thirty minutes or so. Sometimes they'll ask you to come back the next day. Sometimes next week. Sometimes it's simply, "Don't call us, we'll call you." They might. Report to your agent how the audition went, and get on with your life. Sitting by the phone won't make it ring.

Sometimes you're called back because the production team can't agree. Maybe the director wants you, but the producer doesn't. Sometimes they've seen a lot of people and have narrowed it down. They might not even remember which one you are, but they wrote on your résumé, "possible callback." (You'll remind them with an equally great reading.) Many times the preliminary reading was a single scene, and now they're going to want you to read more scenes, some of which will call for different emotions. When there isn't a lot of time, they'll just want you to do the same pages again. They'll probably take more time with you, however, and probably give you some direction, then ask you to do it again.

Should you get a callback:

Remind them of why they called you back in the first place. The people at the callback may be completely different than the people at your first reading. Still, the idea is the same: *You did something right*. They might not remember what it was. Remind them. (No, you don't have to say, "Remember me? I'm the guy who lit your desk on fire.") Unless you have some information to the contrary, wear the same style (better yet, the *same thing*), and read the same material the *same way*. Don't change your approach to the role, unless they ask you to. Of course, when the director starts giving you feedback, go with it.

Don't worry, however, about recreating your original performance so much that you become stale. (If you have completely forgotten what you did at your first audition, then give up trying to recall it, and wing it anew. Your instincts will probably bring you close to what they saw and liked in you the first time anyway.)

Expand on your character. You're not going to do *only* what you did before. Now you're going to deepen your interpretation. Three things can happen at callbacks that are recognized by the casting people, and sometimes talked about among themselves:

One, they can't figure out what in the world attracted them to you in the first place.

Two, you're still interesting to them, but only mildly so, and now they're looking to cull their list further.

Three, you're even more impressive.

> • • •
>
> When I was working on *Friends*, Lisa Kudrow came in several times. Her performance was consistent and funny in each of her callbacks, and we decided to test her at the network. The day before the test, Lisa called and said she had a different "take" on the character and wanted to try it out for us before she went to the network. The producer and I watched this new interpretation, and it was not nearly as funny as her original choice. We thanked her for her initiative, but asked her to forget her new vision of the character and go back to what we'd like so much the first (and second, and third) time she auditioned. She did, and got the part.
>
> —E.K.
>
> • • •

There are going to be more people in the room this time. The chances are they're higher-ups, people who can make, or at least influence, the ultimate decision.

We shouldn't have said that. It's only going to make you nervous. Forget it. It doesn't matter who's in the room.

With the people who read you the first time, be friendly. Respond to, "Good to see you again," with, "Thanks for calling me back." Those people are now nervous, because if you bomb, they've wasted important people's time. There may be as many as a dozen people sitting in on your callback, many of them new faces. Usually the closer to the center, the more important they are, but don't count out the quiet guy in the corner, he could be a sleeper. Play to the whole room.

Almost always you'll read the same scene. There may be some additional scenes to read, but it will usually be as the same character.

If they spring a new character on you—"We think you might be more right for this role"—great. It means they think you're a good actor, and are looking for the right fit in their script. (Don't hesitate to ask for ten minutes outside to look over the new pages and adjust your thinking.)

It may turn out that you're up for more than one role in the production. That's good for you, so enjoy the audition, be flexible and play the different parts as best you can. If you feel really good about one or the other—not just because it's the largest—don't hesitate to say so. But don't be too rigid about it either. You may talk yourself out of a good, if smaller, role.

Don't think just because you're called back you have the role. One hundred or more actors may have been narrowed down to a dozen, but you've still got serious competition. Don't ever take a callback less than very seriously. This could be the closer, so do everything you can to be at your best.

In Short...

- Don't change your approach if they call you back.

. . . .

- Do look at the notes you made from your first audition.
- Do change your approach if given direction.
- Do focus on the reading, not the circumstances.

17

The Chemistry Read

Sometimes the producers will want to check out the chemistry between you and the other actor or actors, often for a male/female project, but also for buddy comedies, family dramas and ensemble shows. This kind of audition usually falls into one of two categories. Either the other role has already been cast—usually with a star—and the producers want to bring in several actors and read them opposite the actor (assuming the star is willing, or interested). Or they've narrowed down several roles to several actors each and want to test various combinations.

Reading with a star presents some special challenges for a lesser known actor. Stars know how to protect themselves. Anyone trying to move up center on stage with an experienced leading man or leading woman will probably find the spot occupied. The larger the star, the more likely he or she will have cast approval in his or her contract. In other words, it doesn't matter how good you are, if they don't like you, you're not going to get their stamp of approval. And even if they don't actually have veto power, the producers are going to ask them about you (it's good politics), and they're not going to be flattering. Not much you can do about this, except, don't say things like, "Oh Mr. Schwarzenegger, I've loved your films ever since I was a little tiny girl," or "Mr. Hackman, my grandfather says your performance in *Bonnie and Clyde* was brilliant." Be courteous, but don't fawn. When it's time to read, play to the actor more than the audience. Pick up on his tempo and ideas of the scene. Try to make them look good.

In series television, you might find yourself opposite a stand-up comic with plenty of jokes but little or no experience in acting. All the more reason to help them out—without, of course, giving away the fact that you know that they don't really know what they're doing. Be as good as you can be without upstaging them.

In sitcoms and other ensemble pieces, it's not uncommon for a chemistry reading to feature several actors the producers are thinking of matching up. They'll probably all be at your level of the business. The key to remember at this one is that the other actors are not your competition. Don't try to out-act them. The producers want to see the chemistry of this group, they want to know if they can count on the two, four or six of you to spark each other's performances. All actors have had the experience of playing with a fellow actor who makes the scene fly, just as all actors have had the experience of playing opposite an actor who is unconscionably self-centered, and feeling the scene sink uncontrollably. At chemistry readings you could face either or both of these experiences. Don't give up. If you're lucky, the producers won't blame you. They'll spot the selfish actors and keep the good ones together.

18

The Suits

Though theatre producers tend to come to final auditions, along with the director and writer, film casting usually has to be approved by studio executives, and television casting usually has to be approved by *both* studio and network executives. Executives don't have the attention span for many auditions. Too many meetings, lunches and phone calls piling up. The casting director will have to arrange an audition for the actors the producer wants to get approval of, and you'll be called back *again*. Don't worry, this is good news. You've made it a long, long way, and the role in that pilot you've always dreamed of may just be yours. What should you do? *Nothing.* You made it this far with the readings you've been giving. Unless you're given some additional direction, just stay on track.

19

The Test Option Deal

If you've made it to the network test for a series regular role, you're going to be asked to sign this version of a contract before your test. The network doesn't want to make you an offer with your agent knowing that you're their first choice. It would put them at a disadvantage in negotiations. The Test Option Deal, or T.O.D., allows the final audition to go forward under conditions that have already been worked out between the studio's Business Affairs department and your agent. There are only two pieces of advice we can give you about this document, and they're probably contradictory.

- One, don't fail to concern yourself with the *business* of acting.
- Two, don't concern yourself with business when you're acting.

On the one hand, an actor who doesn't read his contract deserves to have to meet the terms of the deal. That's a loaded sentence, but not really the purview of this book. So talk to your agent, and *listen to your agent.* Always understand what it is you're signing. If you've been asked to go before the network for a pilot, read the terms of the T.O.D. It will include a fee for the pilot, episode fees, yearly raises should the show be a hit, and lots of things you're paying your agent to think of. (Action figures of you? Personal appearances to open a mall? An out to make a film?) Then, after you've read it and agreed...

Fugedaboutit! Don't go to any audition thinking you don't really want this job, and don't go to any audition dreaming of the big bucks you're going to make when you get it. Go to an audition excited about your performance and the material, and put anything extraneous out of your mind. Focus on the work.

20

The Network Test
and the Screen Test

By the time they're asking for a "test," you know they like you. Again, don't change your approach to the role unless they direct you to. You'll see most of the same people—the producer, director, writer, casting director—plus five to ten more people from the network. Just focus on the work.

They expect you to memorize the dialogue. For feature films, a 35-mm screen test can be the final hurdle. It's expensive for the producers, so if you've been asked to take a true screen test with 35-mm cameras, makeup and wardrobe, lighting and all the goodies—they're very interested. The only key here—beyond preparing what may be the same or a new scene well enough to get "off script"—is this: Don't let the technical aspects throw you. The technicians are there to help you, not get in your way. Be nice to the crew, any one of whom can sabotage you. Work with them, not against them.

Certainly it's time to remember that you're not on a "stage" any longer. Even if all your previous readings were in small rooms, and you were as conversational as can be, there was a "live audience"—if only consisting of a single casting director behind a desk—and your performance was probably a bit more live than it should be in front of a camera. Now you are in front of a camera. Of course, you've taken classes in Acting for the Camera. Now might be a good time to think about those lessons. It's the film or tape that the production team and the executives are going to be looking at to make their final decision.

• • •

Can't act, can't sing, dances a little.

—Studio report on Fred Astaire's first screen test. Really.

• • •

21

Age

"How old are you?"

This is actually an illegal question. You'll hear it, however. Don't point out that they're breaking the law. Know the age of the character you are reading for. That's how old you are. Or tell them the age you've played recently.

If you're under 18, they *do* have a right to ask and a need to know because minors have different working conditions that producers must take into consideration.

22

Nudity

"Why don't you take off your blouse now?"

(Answer: "Because I'm an actress, not a bimbo, you scum-sucking lowlife.") If you unexpectedly hear a request for nudity at an audition, *stop and think.*

First of all, don't ever undress with a video camera in the room. The footage could end up on the Internet, much to your chagrin (and possible career detriment). And with today's micro-camera technology, you never know where there may be a camera.

Second, if there is any nudity required for the role you are auditioning for, your agent should have been informed, and should have passed this information on to you in advance. Only you can decide if you still want to go up for the role.

Third, nudity for a role does not mean nudity at an audition. You might be asked to wear something that shows off your body. Wear a bathing suit or leotard underneath your clothes, if you feel comfortable stripping down to that.

If—and this is really rather rare—you have been informed that the role requires some nudity and that you will be asked to demonstrate your assets at an audition, and *if* you have decided what the hell, Kathleen Turner and Nicole Kidman are doing it (although we doubt they had to audition), then there are steps you should take to protect yourself.

You should—through your agent in advance, or on the spot if you have to—request that there be only a minimum number of people in the room, and that at least one of them be of your sex. You don't want to be alone with anyone in so vulnerable a position, and you want some protection. (Both of you should. A producer who allows an actress to take off her clothes in a closed room with no one else present is leaving himself wide open for a sexual harassment charge, no matter how polite and professional he is.)

We might also say, keep your clothes near by, and don't let anyone come too close to you. But if you've gone this far, you've probably got a steely resolve to make it in this business and don't need a lot of advice from us.

Should you find yourself being physically or emotionally harassed, or offered a role in exchange for sex, leave the office. Report the circumstances to your agent. If you are mistreated, report the circumstances to your agent *and* to law enforcement officials.

23

Offensive Material

It's everywhere. And we're not about to become Language Nazis and define it for you. There are hundreds, if not thousands, of cliché stereotypes in writing. For years it seemed that every musical had to have at least one black maid who stopped the second act with a Big Mama Thornton imitation and if Kenan and Kel aren't *Amos and Andy*, no one is. This is not confined to black characters. Women, Jews, Latinos—every race, creed, class and sexual category is lampooned and caricatured today, including, make that especially, white males. Father hasn't known best in two decades. And it's not getting better, it's getting worse, because sophomoric comedies are easy sells for Hollywood.

If you don't want to support certain kinds of material, whether it's violent, sexual, or racial in nature (you'd be surprised at how many famous actors over the years refuse to swear on film), don't be afraid to say so.

It's best, of course, to pass on the material in advance. If you've been handed a script or sides that seem offensive to you, or that expound ideas you find abhorrent, you can have your agent politely turn down the audition. If you've only just gotten a look at the material while you waited in the outer room for your reading, you'll have to think fast. Either way, the decision is yours, and no casting director will think less of you for turning down an audition.

(Sometimes if the agent simply says "unavailable," your reputation will be enhanced, because everyone will assume you're working!)

It's a bad idea, however, to do the pre-read for the casting director, schedule a callback for the producers, and then show up to tell them you think the material is offensive or beneath you. Obviously they've already committed to the script. Don't wait until the last minute to decide you wouldn't accept a role even if it were offered. This goes for roles you and your agent may decide are too small for you as well. By auditioning, you're saying that you would, assuming a contract can be worked out, like to play the part.

At the same time, don't forget that good ideas are bolstered by good drama, and good drama requires conflict, and conflict requires villains. Playing Adolf Hitler does not make you anti-Semitic. Most actors enjoy a vicarious thrill in playing Evil Personified. Some extremely nice people have carved whole careers out of it.

• • •

Actors Equity once sent out a postcard to its members announcing "Auditions for the All Black Company of *Guys and Dolls*." Appended to the bottom of the notice was the following statement: "All calls will be conducted without regard to race, creed, color or religion."

• • •

And don't leave out the possibility that by playing the role a certain way, you might help deepen the character, or even alter the story's subtext. A good deal of material can probably go either way, depending on your interpretation. If you think there's a possibility there, you might want to discuss it with the director or producer before you accept the role. Be careful. Telling the writer that he's delivered a stereotype is not going to flatter him. You shouldn't be rude or condescending about the material. But you can certainly say—preferably in the middle of an appropriate discussion about the role—that you'd like to make sure you all agree on the approach, because you feel strongly about avoiding offensive stereotypes.

24

Race

"What's your heritage?"

Like, *How old are you?*, this is another question they're not allowed to ask, but often do, usually out of ignorance of the rules. Obviously, you'd like to type yourself into, not out of, the role. Often casting people can't tell the difference between Cuban and Puerto Rican, or Chinese and Taiwanese. In which case, why inform them and risk typing yourself out? You can try to finesse the issue with humor ("Klingon!"), you can say you're whatever race the character is (also called "lying through your teeth"), or you can tell the truth, and hope it's close enough to what they want.

There is in fact no law or union rule that says Laurence Olivier can't play Othello. (He did, in black face, brilliantly.) These days, however, that would draw so much protest from minority self interest groups that producers are loathe to attempt it, for fear of bad publicity.

Although some roles have definable characteristics, many can be quite broad. Years ago, when *Detective Story* by Sidney Kingsley was being cast for its Broadway premiere, Kingsley ran into a black actor he knew on the street. When he mentioned that he was casting his new play, the actor naturally said, "Is there anything in it for me?" Kingsley had to say that there was nothing in it for a black actor. The actor asked why one of the detectives couldn't be black. Kingsley had no real answer, save the general prejudice of the day. He asked the actor to come in and read. The actor got the part, and—for one of the first times in the American theatre—a role in a "white" play (other than a maid or butler) was cast black.

That was the beginning of "non-traditional casting," an issue that has come into greater focus since the civil rights movement. There is even today a non-profit advocacy group—the Non-Traditional Casting Project, or NTCP, that works to encourage the casting of actors of color, those with disabilities, and female actors in roles where race, ethnicity, physical ability or gender are not essential. The NTCP's goal is that one day actors will be cast solely on the basis of individual talent rather than how they conform to stereotypes. Unfortunately, the more generic the character, the less interesting the drama. It is, after all, our cultural differences that define us. Non-traditional casting actually is aimed at *undefined, unspecified* roles. A story set in the Army prior to World War II would not have a black soldier in a white squad, but "a soldier" in any story set since then could be any race. And unless the author specifies, every actor should be given a chance to read.

25

Following the Audition

When it's over, it's over. But remember that you're still auditioning until you're out the door. A few tips for the audition endgame:

- Exit gracefully. Smile, say thanks, and leave as smoothly as you came in. Don't hang around. They won't let you go if they want to hear more, so you can't leave too soon by mistake. You can, however, look like something of an idiot if it takes you two minutes to pack up. (See "don't unpack" when you arrive, Chapter 11.) Don't gather up your coffee, water, re-pack your purse, find your coat, wrap yourself in your scarf and otherwise fumble around while they wait. Anything like that (we know that in New York you might be dressed for snow) should be done in the waiting room, not in front of the casting people during the actual audition.
- Don't apologize. If you think you blew the reading, keep it to yourself. If you're being taped and you really want to start over, just ask to start over. There's nothing wrong with an actor flubbing a line at an audition. At this point, directors are not looking for a perfect performance. They're looking for the character. They're going to assume you can memorize lines, and not expect you to be letter perfect at an audition.

> • • •
>
> Don't overstay your welcome. When you finish with your reading say, "Thank you," and leave. Leave them wanting something more from you. If they want something more, they'll ask you to come back.
>
> —Scott Baio, Actor
>
> • • •

> • • •
>
> Pilot season has got to be the busiest time for everyone in television. As a writer–executive producer there are so many pressures. Meetings with the studio, network, production and of course casting keep us busy 24/7. When actors come in to audition, I appreciate it when they don't feel compelled to make "small talk."
>
> —Bob Stevens
> **Writer-Creator of**
> *Crazy Love*,
> **Co-Executive Producer of**
> *Malcolm in the Middle*
>
> • • •

- Don't ask if you're going to be called back. They probably don't know yet.
- If you're booked for the next two days, or for three days two weeks from now, you may want to mention it as a possible conflict. But don't put them on the spot. Let your agent do that.
- If they don't want to chat, don't. Exit smiling.
- If they have some questions, answer them succinctly. They may simply be making small talk because it's hard to say, "Thanks, now get out." If you're headed for the door too soon, they can always say, "Wait a moment, won't you?"
- Don't be self-deprecating. "Sorry, that was really bad." "I sucked, didn't I?" They may not have thought so. Why put it in their minds?
- And don't forget the key word: Confidence. If you demonstrated it (subtly) coming in, you can demonstrate it going out. They want to see it in the people they hire.

Since we've returned to our main theme, let's examine it a bit more. We think there's a clear difference between *nervousness* and *insecurity*. A young actor who comes in, knees shaking, hands unable to hold the paper steady, voice wobbling, is clearly nervous. Why? Lack of experience, probably, or just a failure to get their nerves under control. Casting people can often see through those nerves. They see it all the time in young, inexperienced, not-yet-jaded performers. Sometimes they can even help the actor get control, by talking a bit, distracting the actor, letting them read once then telling them it was good, now let's do it again without the teeth chattering. Gradually the actor will warm up, and the talent glows. Insecurity, on the other hand, goes much deeper. It's an attitude. And if you're exhibiting it, casting people will see it as a permanent subtext and a sure clue that you won't rise to the occasion.

- We should warn you, just because they applaud doesn't mean you've got the job. If you feel the need to say, "They really liked me," every time you walk out of an audition, that's probably okay. Whatever helps. But casting people really want you to succeed and are often overly polite. One of the traps they fall into is whooping and hollering on your laugh lines, applauding wildly on your song. Sorry to have to warn you about this, but we don't want you to be shocked if you don't get the part.

- There's no harm in warning your agent that you weren't very good. He may be able to salvage your reputation. But don't tell him you were great unless you are very, very sure. You'll make the agent appear clueless to the casting director, which is always a Don't.

• • •

There is an actor who I have auditioned and hired many times. He has worked often over the years in both television and film. He always had a casualness and confidence when he auditioned that I respected. One day I was auditioning him for the producer and director. He read, did a nice job, and left. The director asked me to try to get him back to give him an adjustment. As I ran out to the parking lot (please walk slowly when you are leaving an audition—this happens all the time). I asked him if he would please come back to read some more. He asked for another set of sides. I asked him what he did with his sides, and he explained that part of his process was to rip up the sides after every audition. This helped him forget about each audition, so he could move on and concentrate on either the next audition or the next job. Every actor needs to find his/her own way of letting go of the audition.

—E.K.

• • •

- Don't mope. You should have already planned something for after the audition that you will enjoy. An acting, singing, or dancing class is good. That can help remind you that you're still an actor, even if you were turned down. An evening with friends could bolster your confidence, and you'll get a chance to dish the casting people who failed to appreciate you. Treat yourself to a movie (unless it features a role you lost). You did your preparation, and gave the best audition you were capable of. Move on. You're going to go on a lot of auditions, and you're going to feel rejected at many of them. Do not let auditions become a daily humiliation. They are part and parcel of your job, whether you scored a role or not. Let it go.

In Short...

- Don't apologize if you think you gave a bad audition.

. . . .

- Do put the audition behind you.

26

A Few Final Words

HOW MANY TIMES SHOULD I AUDITION FOR THE SAME ROLE?

Once upon a time, producers and directors dithered so much, and called actors back so often, that finally the actor's unions for both stage and screen negotiated a limit to the number of times you can be auditioned for the same project without being paid for your time. Each contract is different, but if you find yourself being called back for the umpteenth time, check with your agent or union.

FEEDBACK

It's your agent's job to get feedback on your auditions, if possible. Some casting directors will tell your agent what they thought. Some honestly, some vaguely. Don't call the casting director yourself, it puts them on the spot. But feedback can be enormously helpful. Don't hesitate to check in with your agent on the subject. Be prepared to hear the truth, though you may not like it.

THANK-YOU NOTES

They might seem a little gratuitous, but it's an ingratiating business. A specific thank you note to the casting director who first brought you in for the role, whether you got the part or not, can be useful. Remember, it might be months since they spoke to you. Reminding them that you're available again won't hurt. If you got the job and completed it successfully, no harm in telling the producer and the director you enjoyed working with them. Frankly, they should be thanking you, but hey, it's all about networking.

POSTCARDS

This is a good way to remind people about yourself. A postcard to the casting director, which happens to have your picture on it, might sit on their desk for a few days.

For that matter, you should "keep in touch" with casting directors you have worked with or auditioned for in the past. Phone calls are not appreciated. The sheer number can overwhelm and annoy casting offices. The postcard is best. If you change agencies, by all means send casting directors a postcard. If you have a new headshot, it won't hurt to ask them to "update their files" with your new picture and résumé. If you've been on location for a lengthy stay, tell them you're back and available.

Be careful about overdoing it. Unless you have a specific reason, every three to six months is probably about as often as even a hard-working, self-promoting actor can get away with. If you're constantly seen as looking for work, you're probably also seen as an actor who isn't getting much of it, and they're going to start to wonder why.

Of course, if you book a job, you'll want to tell everyone you know to watch, or buy a ticket. Particularly casting directors. This is a great excuse to send out postcards with particulars of the broadcast date, time and channel, or the film's premiere schedule.

THE DEAL MEMO

There's more to acting than auditioning—though sometimes it doesn't seem like it—and we'd like to leave you with a few more Do's and Don'ts.

In the theatre, you may go directly to the contract negotiations. In Hollywood, the Deal Memo is a preliminary step, and it's pretty much as binding as a contract—in fact, it may look like an elaborate contract or it may appear as a simple letter. Although your agent will negotiate it with the casting director, you must be cognizant of your arrangements. Don't rely on other people to protect you in shark-infested waters. A few things you should know about the deal memo:

- "Start Date" can be very specific. It can also read "o/a" and a date, which stands for "on or about." This gives the producers leeway of a day either way, which is often necessary, should the production's schedule change at the last minute. Which it almost always does. Producers have to specify the date seven days in advance. This doesn't mean you will definitely be working on your first contracted day. Your scene might not be filming. But that's the day you must be available. The "o/a" notation is not allowed on day-player contracts.

- "Salary" is always specific. What you see is what you're going to get, minus taxes and agent's commissions, usually of 10 percent, though managers often take 15. "Scale plus 10" is a common negotiating ploy for actors without an established price. It means union scale plus enough extra for your agent so your salary doesn't fall below union scale. (Though of course, with taxes, it will.) "Scale plus 10" is not, by the way, and contrary to popular belief, required. You might have an agent (10 percent), a manager (15 percent), a business manager (5 percent), a lawyer (5 percent) and a press rep (5 percent) on your payroll. Your union doesn't care. Nor does the producer. "Scale," that is, whatever the minimum salary is for that job under that contract at that time—among most unions this is known as the "Minimum Basic Agreement"—is the only minimum your union requires.

- "Guaranteed Days." All SAG contracts include pay-or-play, which means that even if the film is canceled or the role cut before you shoot it, you get paid. How many days depends on this clause. If the shooting schedule goes over, you will have to be paid on a pro-rated basis for the extra days. By the same token, you're guaranteeing them days. Don't book eight days if you've only got a window of three.

There are, of course, myriad details in a good contract. What will your billing be? If the production goes out of town, what will your transportation, housing and per diem (extra money each day for food and expenditures) be? Do you participate in any profits? Syndication? All this and more should be negotiated by your agent. Stay in touch with him on these details. Make it clear if you have things you particularly want. Review them before you sign. Remember, your agent is not going to have to fulfill this contract. You are.

"When will I hear if I got the part?"

You probably won't, unless you badger your agent to find out, or read in *Variety* that the show started rehearsing without you. We know it's frustrating to give a good audition, then not hear anything. No one is trying to test your patience. They either haven't made up their minds yet, or they have, and everyone is too busy to tell you. Most casting offices are just too busy to call everyone's agent back and report on an actor. They'll do this occasionally when they particularly want the agent to know that the actor's audition was much appreciated, but he just didn't quite fit what they wanted this time. And they'll respond if the agent asks them. Agents often check in with casting directors to see if the actors they sent fit the bill, and in doing so may discover that their initial vision of the role was incorrect. If so, they'll offer to send over some different actors. This can happen simply because the original descriptions were vague, or a role has changed direction. Agents are busy too, and once they've secured an audition, there's usually not much more they can do. Sometimes a persistent agent can get the ear of a casting director, producer or director just after a client's audition, to see how he did. If the agent senses some vacillation, he'll pitch the client's talents, offer to send over more tape and, by working on the director's indecisiveness, wangle another reading. But not often. Good agents are persistent, but know very well they can be annoying, and don't want to step over the line. An agent usually hears, one way or the other, because other clients in the office may have booked the job.

"I had two good auditions last week and haven't heard yet. Should I go on vacation?"

Yes. But keep in touch.

"Should I crash an audition?"

No. Never. It's happened, and actors have been allowed to read. Trouble is, nine times out of ten, they've not only been thrown out on their ears, but they've made an enemy of that particular casting director, pissed off their own agent, *and* left the impression that they have more moxie than talent. In Hollywood, it's hard to find out the location of auditions, and you risk your life sneaking onto a studio lot in this post 9/11 climate. In both New York and L.A. auditions are tightly scheduled. Crashing an audition is a very bad idea that is likely to hurt your career.

Many actors who don't audition well discover that they have been bringing anger into the audition with them. This is certainly forgivable. Getting rejected all the time by people who may have less talent than you do, some of whom can be downright rude, can

• • •

When I was a stagestruck college student, a professional actor lectured in the theatre department. He spoke wisely and wittily about the business of the theatre, all those things we hadn't heard about as we practiced our diction, pantomime, and makeup. But his primary pitch was this: *Don't do it. It's too hard, too debilitating. You'll throw your life away waiting for other people to decide your fate. If there is anything else you can do, do it.* Later, when a stalwart few followed him to the cafeteria and sat with him over lunch, we asked if he really meant it. How could he, a working actor, then touring with a wonderful comedy at the largest downtown theatre, dash our dreams so thoroughly? "I thought it was my duty to try to talk you out of it," he said. "Because if you're someone who can be talked out of going into the theatre, then you shouldn't go into the theatre. You won't have the fortitude."

—D.M.F.

• • •

build up a lot of hostility. The endless rounds of auditions and rejections you'll face as a new, young actor in town will come as quite a shock to anyone who had the lead role in their school play every year for the last four years. You've got to let anger and hostility go, however, if you are to audition well. One of the best ways to do that is to see the audition as a chance to practice your craft.

- Once you've finished the audition, put it behind you. Don't hang on to the fact that they *might* call you back. Don't pester them or your agent. Move on to the next one.

See each individual audition as only part of an overall process. Many actors have failed to earn a role at an audition, only to find out that everyone liked them very much, that their reputation was immeasurably enhanced, and sooner or later, a good part was theirs.

In Short...

- Don't ignore what you are signing—whether with an agent, a producer, a studio, or network.

- Don't fail to get your agent to ask for feedback.

- Don't ever crash an audition.

. . . .

- Do read your contract.

- Do send postcards to keep in touch.

27

First Day on the Job

As you begin your career, you might want to try to wrangle a job as an extra, intern, or production assistant on any set you can. That way, when you land an acting job, you'll already know the lay of the land. There's an etiquette to working on a set, and it won't hurt to experience it. You'll look intelligent to the production crew if you're familiar with the lingo and procedures.

If you lack "on set" experience, simply use your common sense. If it's your first day on the set, don't be too timid to ask questions. ("Should I go to wardrobe? Where is it?") There are plenty of assistant directors and production assistants standing around, dying to look busy. Make friends with them. You may very well have done a fair amount of theatre in high school or college, but perhaps not film work. When they ask you to "hit your mark," you'll want to know what they're talking about.

- We could warn you to be on time, be sober and be polite, but some actors are none of these things and are still very successful. Nevertheless, if you want a long career, behaving professionally is a major factor.
- Respect everyone on the set, from the director to the interns. Not all sets are pleasant. Murphy's Law (anything that can go wrong, will) works overtime in film production, and stress levels go up. Maintain a professional approach.

- This isn't the Moscow Art Theatre. (For the uninitiated, they often rehearsed for months, gradually adding sets and costumes, improvising and experimenting until they settled into very realistic performances.) This is New York or Hollywood. You've got to deliver. In Hollywood, you've got to deliver *now*. In the theatre, you're sometimes going to have a luxurious amount of time to prepare a role (up to six weeks rehearsal for a Broadway show), and sometimes frighteningly little (entire musical comedies are mounted in five days in summer stock, while the same actors perform another musical at night). A half-hour television sitcom usually rehearses like a play, but may have only three days of rehearsal and a day of camera blocking before shooting. Films and one hour television shows rarely rehearse at all, the actors and director grab what time they can between set-ups, a situation that often comes as something of a shock to theatre actors recruited to Hollywood. Whatever the situation, remember that producers and directors are *nervous people.* You don't have too long to convince them you're going to be great. While this situation is virtually anti-art, the fact is, as an actor, *you're always auditioning.* No one expects you to be brilliant at a cold table reading, but actors who signed to guest on a sitcom have been known to be fired at lunch time of the first day, due to the fact that they walked through the table read. (Usually fooled into doing so by the series' regulars, who usually do walk through most of their table reads and rehearsals. But they have their parts down, and the producers know what they're going to do.)

  This is a dilemma we can't help you with much, except to warn you. Depending on the situation, you may not have much time. You were hired based on your audition. Producers expect you to start there and grow further. Actors who start from scratch at the first rehearsal by stripping themselves of any characteristics whatsoever and building a character up slowly and organically (and don't get us wrong, it's a great technique) might have to re-think their approach under certain less-than-luxurious circumstances. Let's just say this. Your technique doesn't have to change—it must be good, you got the job. But you might have to go through the process a bit faster.

We hope a good part will be yours. In the meantime, one last piece of advice:

Love the little trade which thou hast learned,
and be content therewith.

> —*Marcus Aurelius Antoninus*

FOR THE ACTOR

HOW TO AGENT YOUR AGENT
by Nancy Rainford

Nancy Rainford takes the reader behind the scenes to reveal the techniques, politics and unspoken rules of agenting. Agents and managers are the gatekeepers and power brokers to getting work in Hollywood. With an easy style, Rainford candidly delivers fresh insight into the mechanics and motivation of agents and managers at work. Get the tools you need to protect yourself, build a career, and train your agent to work for YOU. Filled with industry anecdotes, uncensored descriptions and accounts of show-biz players, Rainford gives you the advice and know-how you will wish you'd learned years ago.
$17.95, ISBN 1580650422

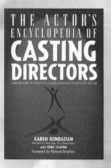

THE ACTOR'S ENCYCLOPEDIA OF CASTING DIRECTORS
Interviews with Over 100 Casting Directors on How to Get the Job
by Karen Kondazian with Eddie Shapiro, foreword by Richard Dreyfuss

Kondazian has compiled insider information and intimate profiles from talking to premier casting directors in film, television, theatre and commercials from Los Angeles to New York. Casting directors speak on the record to reflect and convey expert advice about how to get in the door and how to prepare effectively for readings. Find out from casting directors what's hot and what's not.
$19.95, ISBN 1580650139

HOW TO GET THE PART... WITHOUT FALLING APART!
Featuring the Haber Phrase Technique® for Actors
by Margie Haber with Barbara Babchick, foreword by Heather Locklear

Acting coach to the stars Margie Haber has created a revolutionary phrase technique to get actors through readings without stumbling over the script. The book helps actors break through the psychological roadblocks to auditioning with a 10-step method for breaking down the scene. Actors learn to prepare thoroughly, whether they have twenty minutes or two weeks. Includes celebrity photos and audition stories.
$17.95, ISBN 1580650147

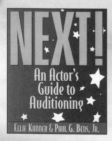

NEXT! AN ACTOR'S GUIDE TO AUDITIONING
by Ellie Kanner and Paul G. Bens, Jr.

Written by two of Hollywood's hottest casting directors, *NEXT!* is the definitive insider's guide to successfully navigating the complicated maze of auditions and landing that all-important role in a movie or TV show. *NEXT!* details the common errors that most inexperienced actors make when auditioning.
ISBN 0943728711, $19.95

FOR THE ACTOR

MAKING MONEY IN VOICE-OVERS
Winning Strategies to a Successful Career in TV, Commercials, Radio and Animation
by Terri Apple, foreword by Gary Owens

This book helps the actor, radio DJ, vocal impressionist or amateur cartoon voice succeed in voice-overs, no matter where you live. From assessing one's competitive advantages to creating a demo tape to handling initial sessions, Apple provides a clear guide full of insider tips and strategies helpful to both beginners and experienced professionals.
$16.95, ISBN 1580650112

THE ACTOR'S GUIDE TO PERFORMING SHAKESPEARE
by Madd Harold

Madd Harold strips Shakespeare of his mystique and gives the professional actor, drama student and theatre director access to unambiguous and easy-to-master techniques used by great actors throughout the ages. Includes practice exercises and a selection of twenty-two new and unexpected Shakespearean monologues that casting directors won't already know by rote.
$18.95, ISBN 1580050405

HOLLYWOOD REPRESENTATION DIRECTORY, 26th Edition

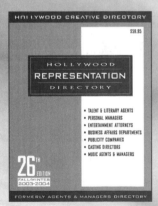

- Over 6,500 names of agents and managers
- Over 1,500 talent and literary agencies and management companies coast to coast
- Includes addresses, phone and fax numbers, staff names and titles, and submission policies
- Cross-referenced indices by name and type
- Film and TV Casting Directors and Publicity Companies
- Published every April and October

Single issue	$59.95
1-year print subscription	$99.95
2-year print subscription	$189.95

FOR THE SCREENWRITER

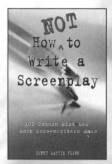

HOW NOT TO WRITE A SCREENPLAY
101 Common Mistakes Most Screenwriters Make
by Denny Martin Flinn

Having read tons of screenplays as an executive, Denny Martin Flinn has come to understand that while all good screenplays are unique, all bad screenplays are the same. Flinn's book will teach the reader how to avoid the pitfalls of bad screenwriting, and arrive at one's own destination intact. Every example used is gleaned from a legitimate screenplay. Flinn's advice is a no-nonsense analysis of the latest techniques for crafting first-rate screenplays that sell.
$16.95, ISBN 1580650155

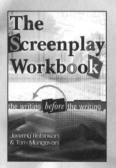

THE SCREENPLAY WORKBOOK:
The Writing Before the Writing
by Jeremy Robinson and Tom Mungovan

Every time a screenwriter sits down to write a screenplay, he has to grapple with the daunting question of, "Where do I start?" The preparation time, or the writing *before* the writing, can be intimidating. *The Screenplay Workbook* is an instructional manual combined with proprietary worksheets, charts and fill-in lists designed to give screenwriters a better way to focus on the task of writing a screenplay. All of the organization is done, the right questions are asked, the important subjects are covered.
$18.95, ISBN 1580650538

ELEMENTS OF STYLE FOR SCREENWRITERS
The Essential Manual for Writers of Screenplays
by Paul Argentini

Paul Argentini presents an essential reference masterpiece in the art of clear and concise principles of screenplay formatting, structure and style for screenwriters. Argentini explains how to design and format manuscripts to impress any film school professor, story editor, agent, producer or studio executive. A to Z listing of format terms and examples. Includes a special section on stage play formatting.
$11.95, ISBN 1580650031

POWER SCREENWRITING
The 12 Stages of Story Development
by Michael Chase Walker

Michael Chase Walker offers a clear and straightforward framework upon which to build story plots. Standing on the broad shoulders of Joseph Campbell, Christopher Vogler, and others who have demonstrated how mythology is used, Walker brings passion, insight and clarity to a whole new range of story traditions never before examined. Walker offers a wide variety of alternative principles and techniques that are more flexible, adaptable and relevant for the modern storyteller. This book gives insight into the art of storytelling as a way to give depth and texture to any screenplay.
$19.95, ISBN 1580650414

FOR THE SCREENWRITER

THE COMPLETE WRITER'S GUIDE TO HEROES & HEROINES
Sixteen Master Archetypes
by Tami D. Cowden, Caro LaFever, Sue Viders

By following the guidelines of the archetypes presented in this comprehensive reference work, writers can create extraordinarily memorable characters and elevate their writing to a higher level. The authors give examples of well-known heroes and heroines from television and film so the reader can picture the archetype in his or her mind. The core archetype tells the writer how heroes or heroines think and feel, what drives them and how they reach their goals.
$17.95, ISBN 1580650244

WRITING SHORT FILMS
Structure and Content for Screenwriters
by Linda J. Cowgill

Contrasting and comparing the differences and similarities between feature films and short films, screenwriting professor Linda Cowgill offers readers the essential tools necessary to make their writing crisp, sharp and compelling. Emphasizing characters, structure, dialogue and story, Cowgill dispels the "magic formula" concept that screenplays can be constructed by anyone with a word processor and a script formatting program.
$19.95, ISBN 0943728800

SECRETS OF SCREENPLAY STRUCTURE
How to Recognize and Emulate the Structural Frameworks of Great Films
by Linda J. Cowgill

Linda Cowgill articulates the concepts of successful screenplay structure in a clear language, based on the study and analysis of great films from the thirties to present day. *Secrets of Screenplay Structure* helps writers understand how and why great films work, and how great form and function can combine to bring a story alive.
$16.95, ISBN 158065004X

THIS BUSINESS OF SCREENWRITING
How to Protect Yourself as a Screenwriter
by Ron Suppa

Practical tips for the writer, with advice on crafting marketable treatments, pitches, spec screenplays and adaptations. Plus important information on how to protect your work, get representation, make deals and more! Calling on his years of experience as both a buyer and seller of screenplays, Suppa conveys a taste of the real world of professional screenwriting to help writers survive and thrive in the sometimes messy collision of art and business.
$19.95, ISBN 1580650163

FOR THE FILMMAKER

THE IFILM DIGITAL VIDEO FILMMAKER'S HANDBOOK
by Maxie D. Collier

Maxie Collier's book covers the creative and technical aspects of digital shooting and is designed to provide detailed, practical information on DV filmmaking. Collier delves into the mechanics and craft of creating personal films and introduces the reader to the essential terminology, concepts, equipment and services required to produce a quality DV feature film. Includes DVD.
$24.95, ISBN 1580650317

THE INDIE PRODUCER'S HANDBOOK
Creative Producing from A to Z
by Myrl A. Schreibman

Myrl Schreibman has written a straightforward, insightful and articulate account of what it takes to make a successful feature film. Filled with engaging and useful anecdotes, Schreibman provides a superlative introduction and overview to all the key elements of producing feature films. Useful to film students and filmmakers as a theoretical and practical guide to understanding the filmmaking process.
$21.95, ISBN 1580650376

FILM PRODUCTION
The Complete *UNCENSORED* Guide to Independent Filmmaking
by Greg Merritt

Merritt cuts through the fluff and provides the reader with real-world facts about producing and selling a low-budget motion picture. Topics covered include: pre-production, principal photography, post-production, distribution, script structure and dialogue, raising money, limited partnerships, scheduling and budgeting, cast and crew, production equipment, scoring, publicity, festivals, foreign distribution, video and more.
$24.95, ISBN 0943728991

THE ULTIMATE FILM FESTIVAL SURVIVAL GUIDE, 2ND EDITION
by Chris Gore

Learn the secrets of successfully marketing and selling your film at over 600 film festivals worldwide. Author Chris Gore reveals how to get a film accepted and what to do after acceptance, from putting together a press kit to putting on a great party to actually closing a deal. Gore includes an expanded directory section, new interviews as well as a new chapter that details a case study of the most successful independent film to date, *The Blair Witch Project*.
$19.95, ISBN 1580650325